Writing is Life

200 Therapeutic Journaling Prompts

Soneakqua J. White

Copyright © 2018 by Soneakqua J. White

All rights reserved.

No part of this book may be reproduced or transmitted in any form or by any means, electronic or mechanical, including photocopying, recording, or by any information storage and retrieval system, without permission in writing from the copyright author, except for the use of brief quotations in a book review.

Published in the United States by
Pen2Pad Ink Publishing.

ISBN: 9781732209497

Requests to publish work from this book or to contact the author should be sent to:
sjw@atthetablecounseling.com

Soneakqua J. White retains the rights to all images

Cover Art Created By: Mary Sweeney Howe

Interior Design: Pen2Pad Ink Publishing

Disclaimer:

This journal belongs to

_____.

If you are reading this, you have violated my right to privacy and you are now treading in dangerous territory. Your best option is to close this book now. If I feel the need to share the personal contents of this book with you I will do so in my own time and in my own way. Should you choose to proceed your feelings will likely be hurt. You are viewing this without my permission and I will neither recant, nor will I apologize for any statement that may offend you. Continue at your own risk. You have been warned...

As a therapist, I challenge most of my clients to write. I do this for several reasons. One, because it's cathARTic! It helps release thoughts, feelings and emotions that you are keeping bottled up. Two, it helps me to get a better understanding of what direction we may need to go in therapeutically. And three, it often brings revelation for many. Meaning it can reveal things that you did not realize you were holding or had maybe even suppressed or repressed.

This activity book is not meant to take the place of a therapist if you need one. It is designed to get you started with journaling, keep you on track and to be utilized as a coping mechanism. There is no need to complete every single prompt. Use them at your discretion but challenge yourself to be honest and thorough. Do not be afraid to seek help if you discover that you have unresolved issues that you cannot resolve on your own. Write often and write faithfully!

Sunshine! Talk about one great thing that has happened to you.

If money and time were not factors, where would you be right now?

Talk about someone you need to forgive.

Write about 3 things you are grateful for.

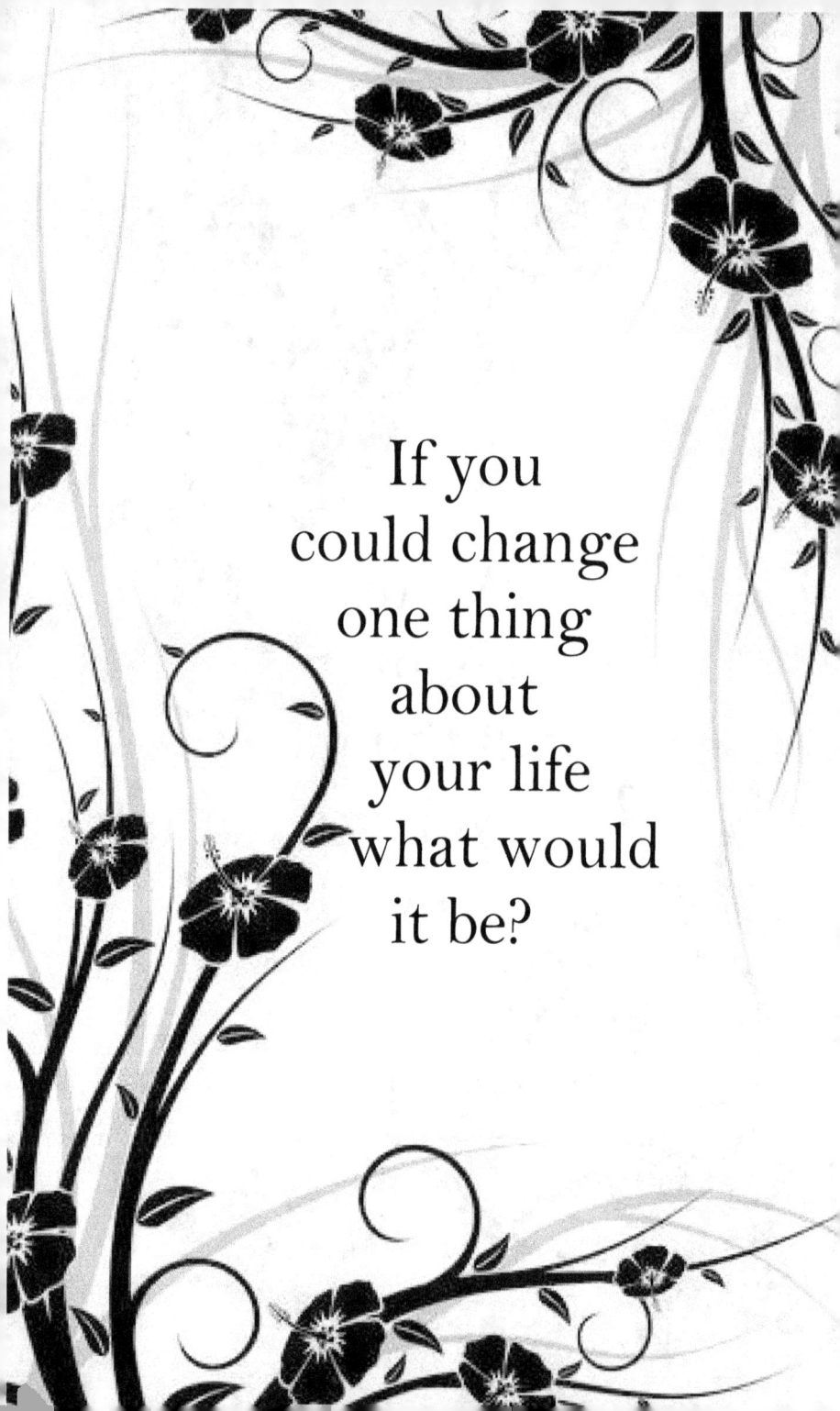

Tell
me
about
something
that
makes
you
happy.

Describe the last nightmare you remember.

If you could have a do-over in life, where would you restart?

If you won the lottery what would you do with the money?

Talk about someone who has been an inspiration in your life.

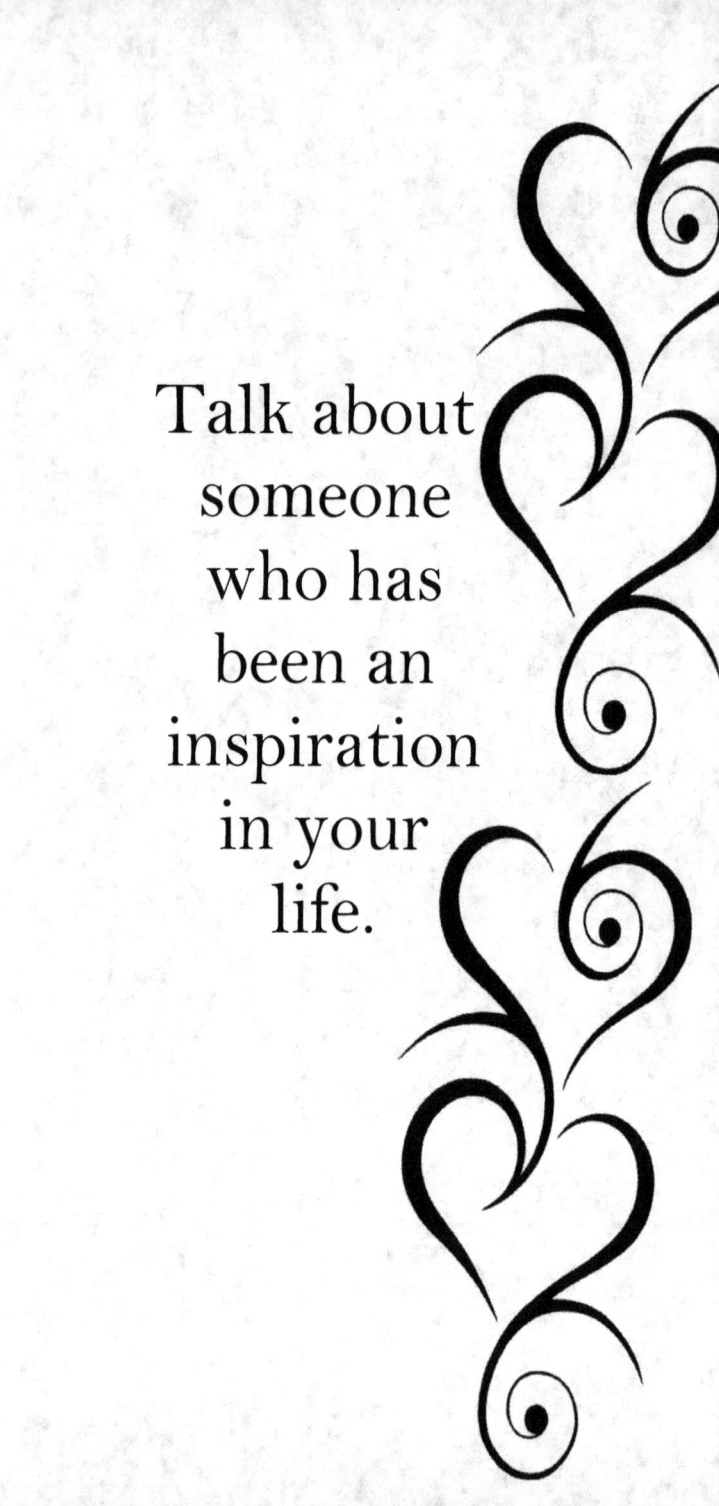

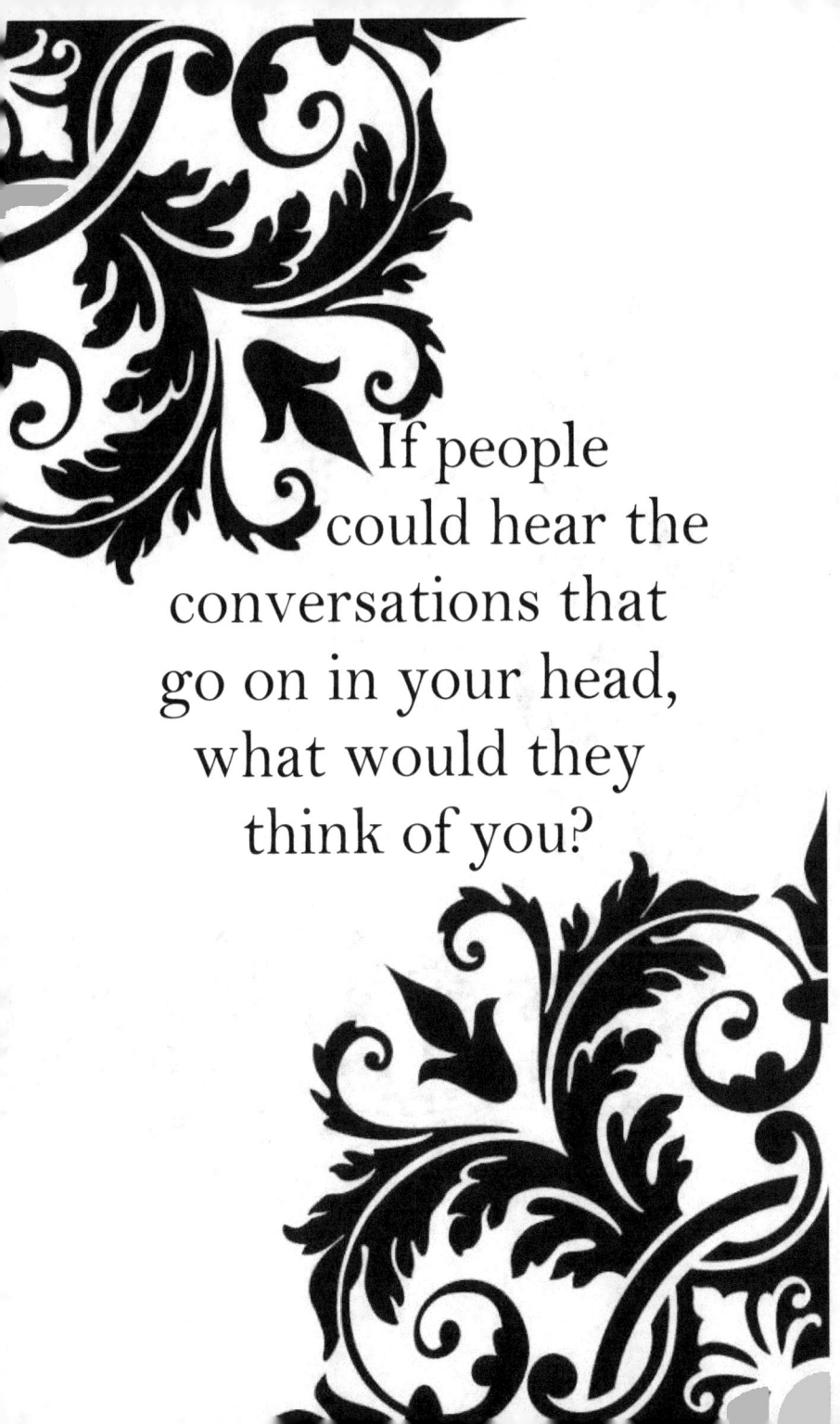

Describe your best friend.

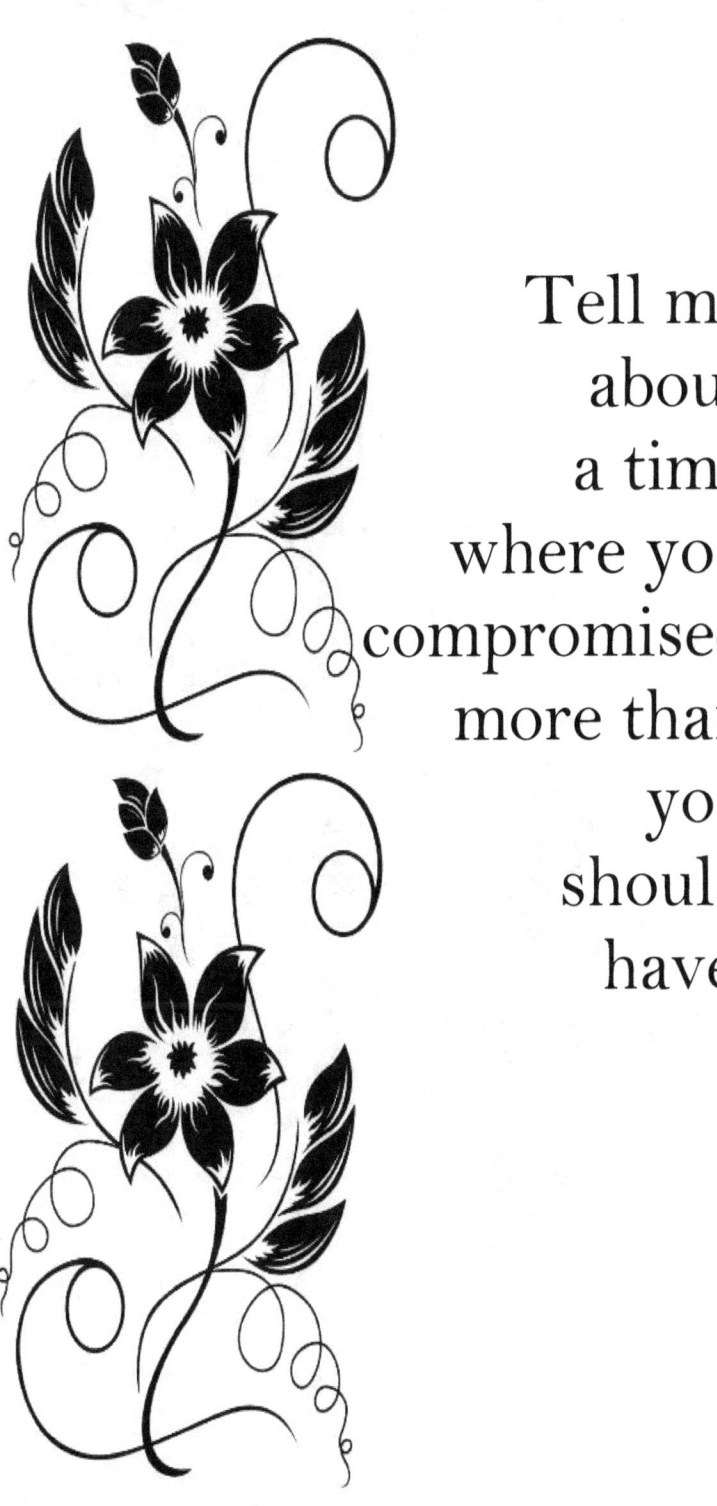

Tell me about a time where you compromised more than you should have.

What's your favorite junk food and why?

When you were a kid, what did you want to be when you grew up and why?

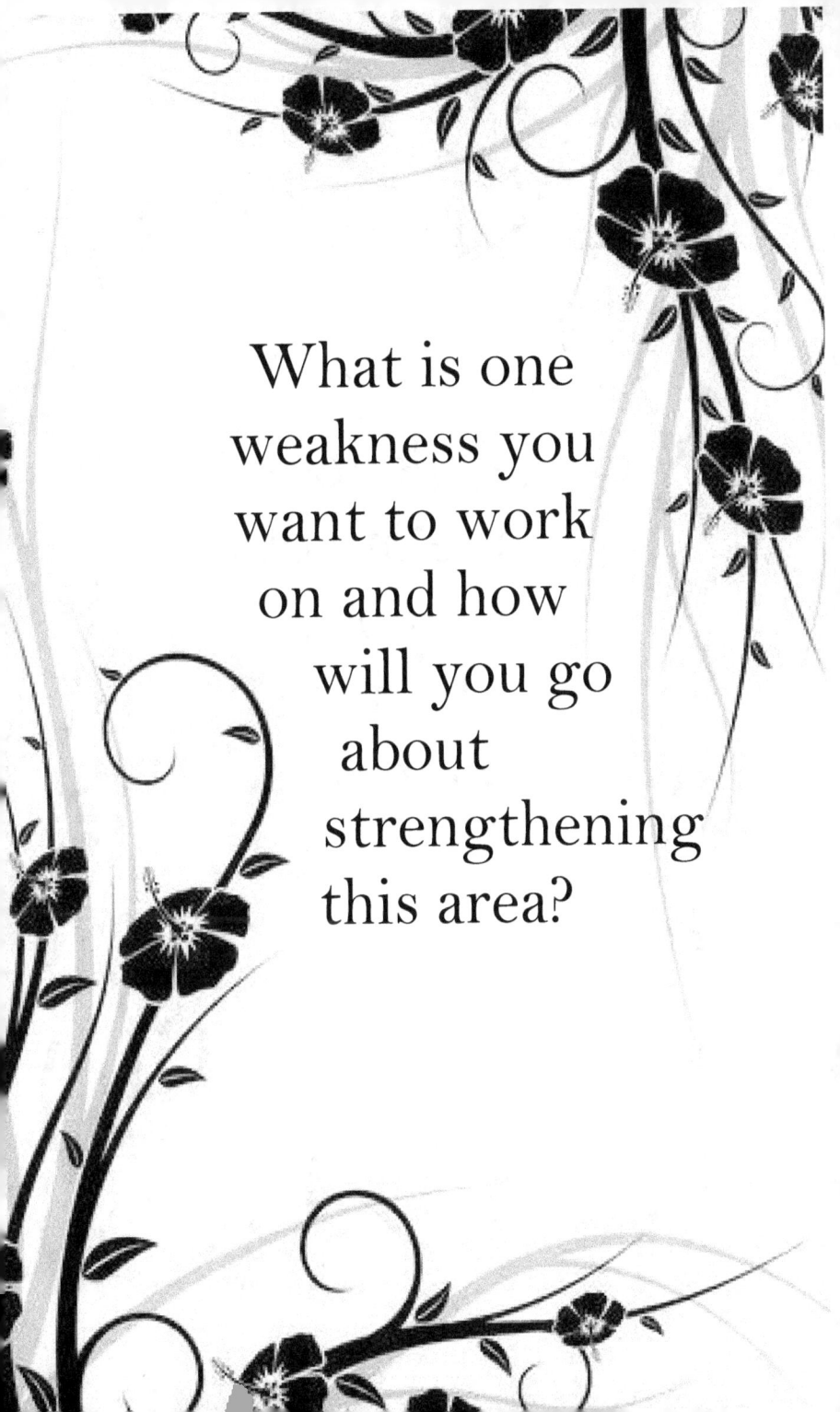

What is one weakness you want to work on and how will you go about strengthening this area?

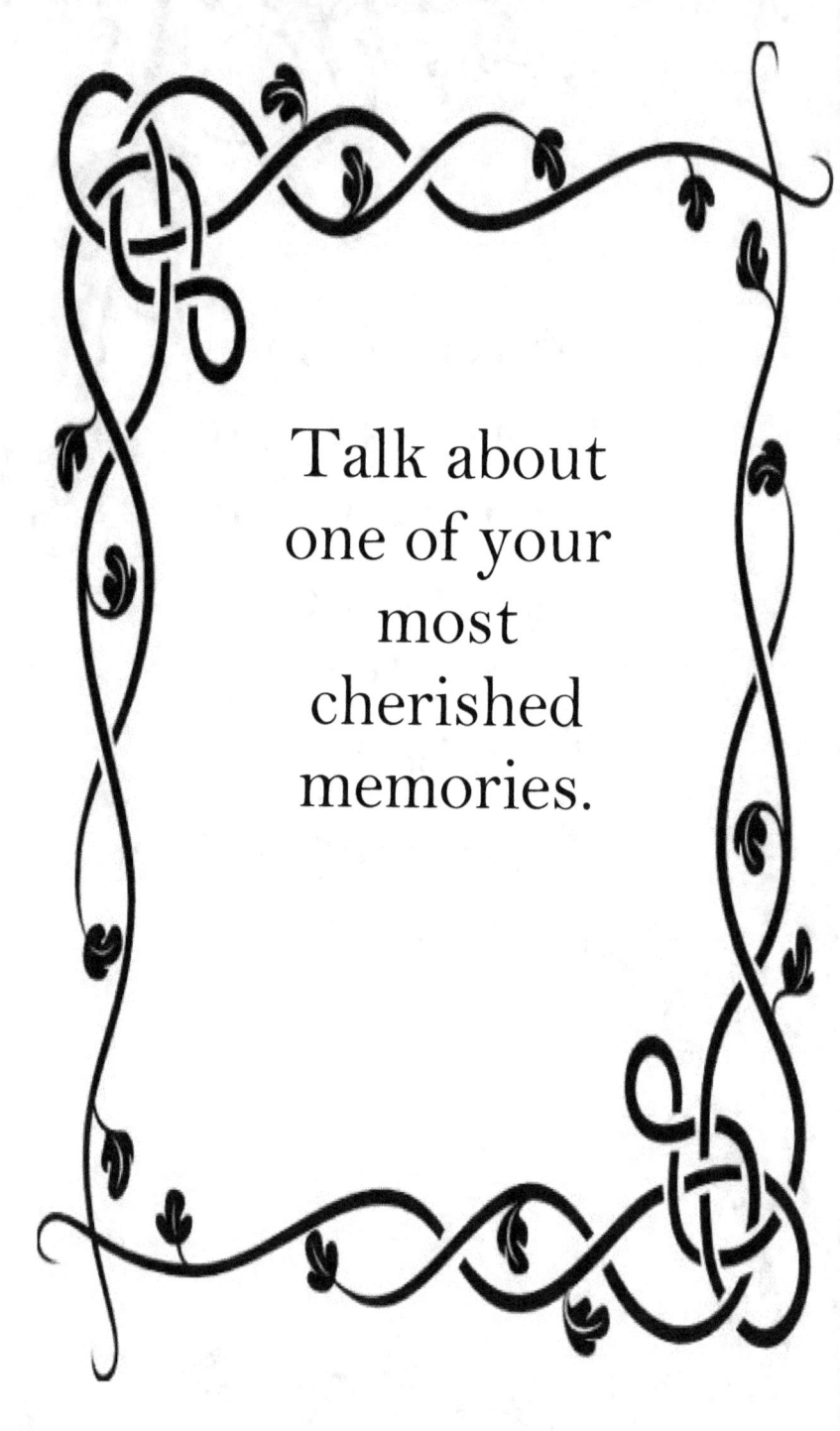

Talk about one of your most cherished memories.

If today was your last day on Earth, what would you want to make sure to do?

Tell me about something you used to do that you don't do anymore.

Name a place you'd like to visit and why.

If you could tell God anything right now, what would you say?

Tell me about the last time you were angry.

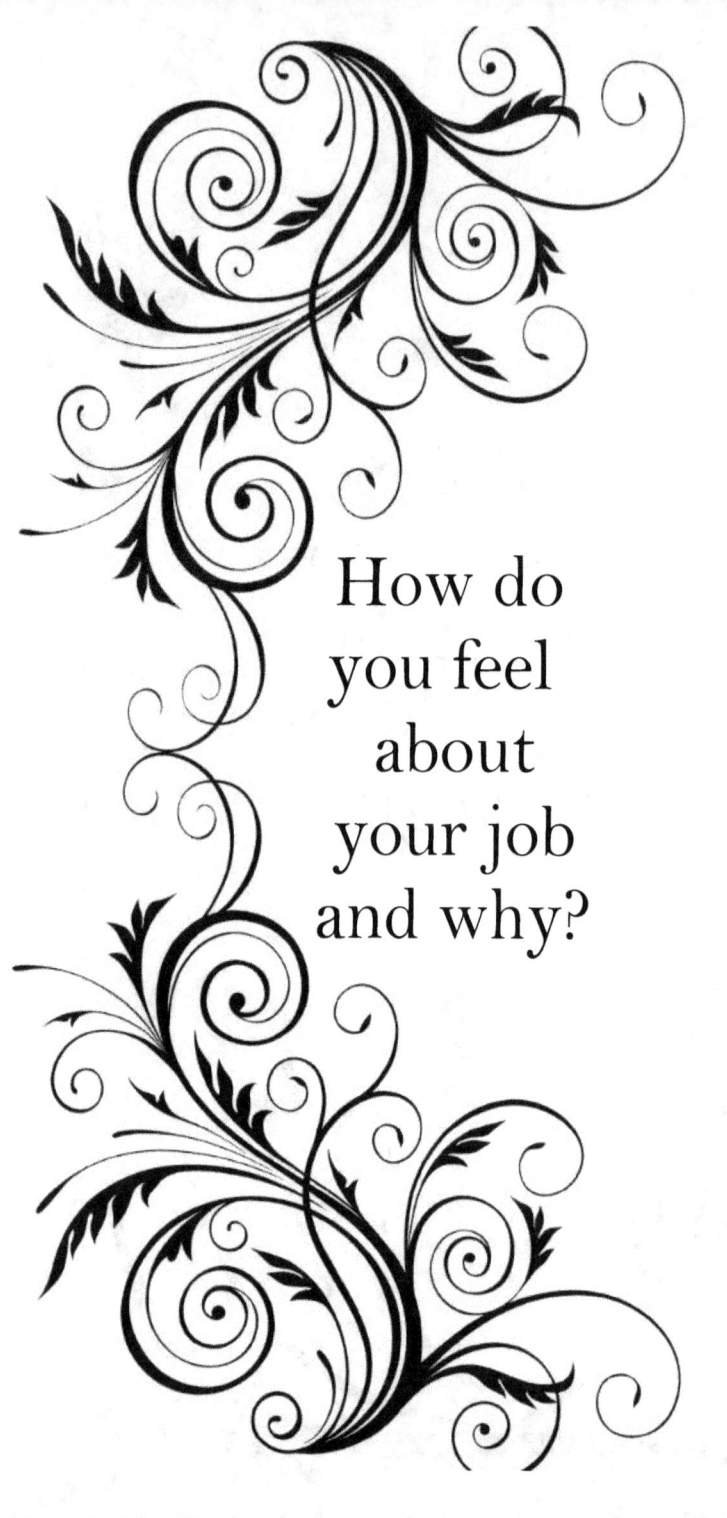

Tell me about something you lost that you want back.

Look into a full-length mirror and describe what you see.

Describe your work environment.

When someone wrongs you, what should they do to try and make it up to you?

Tell me one thing that cheers you up when you're sad.

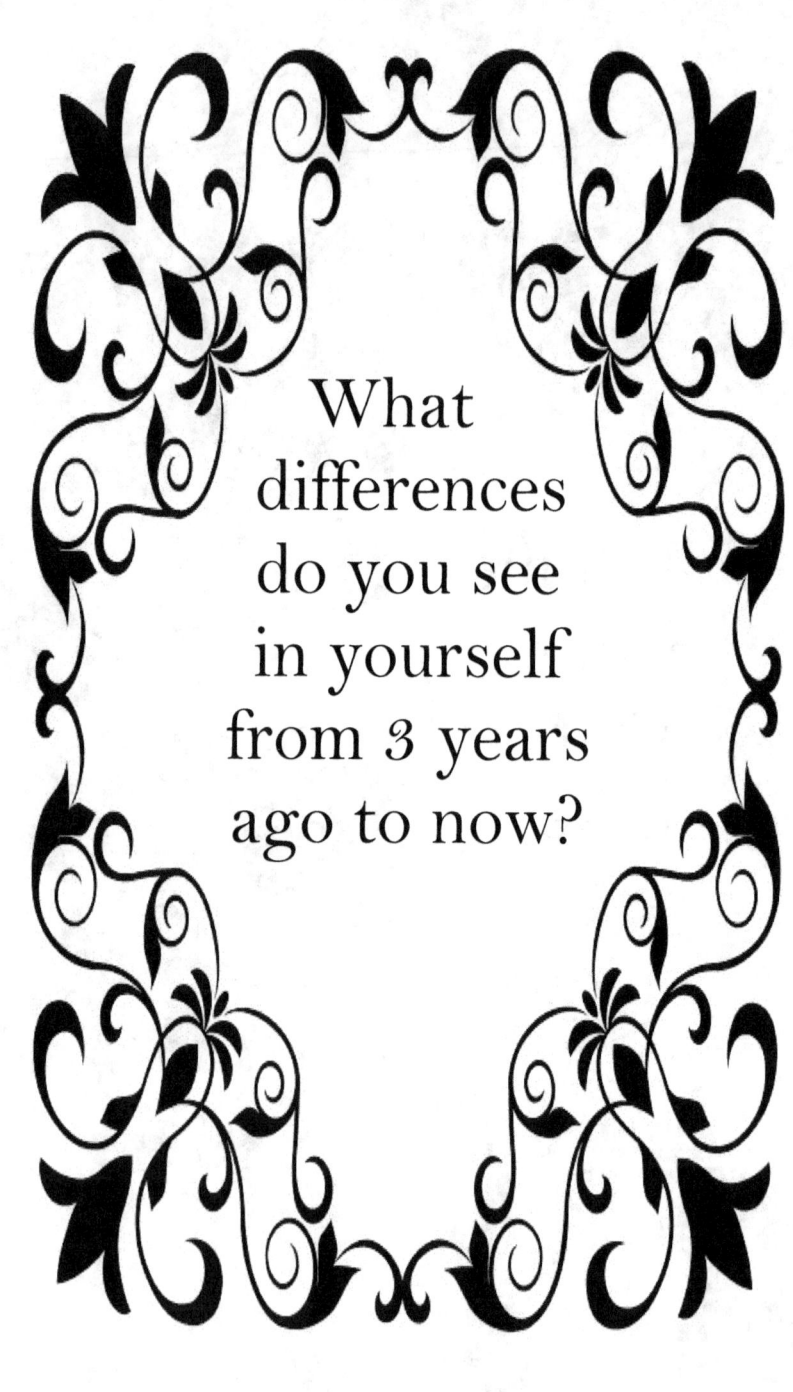

What differences do you see in yourself from 3 years ago to now?

How do you feel about having sex?

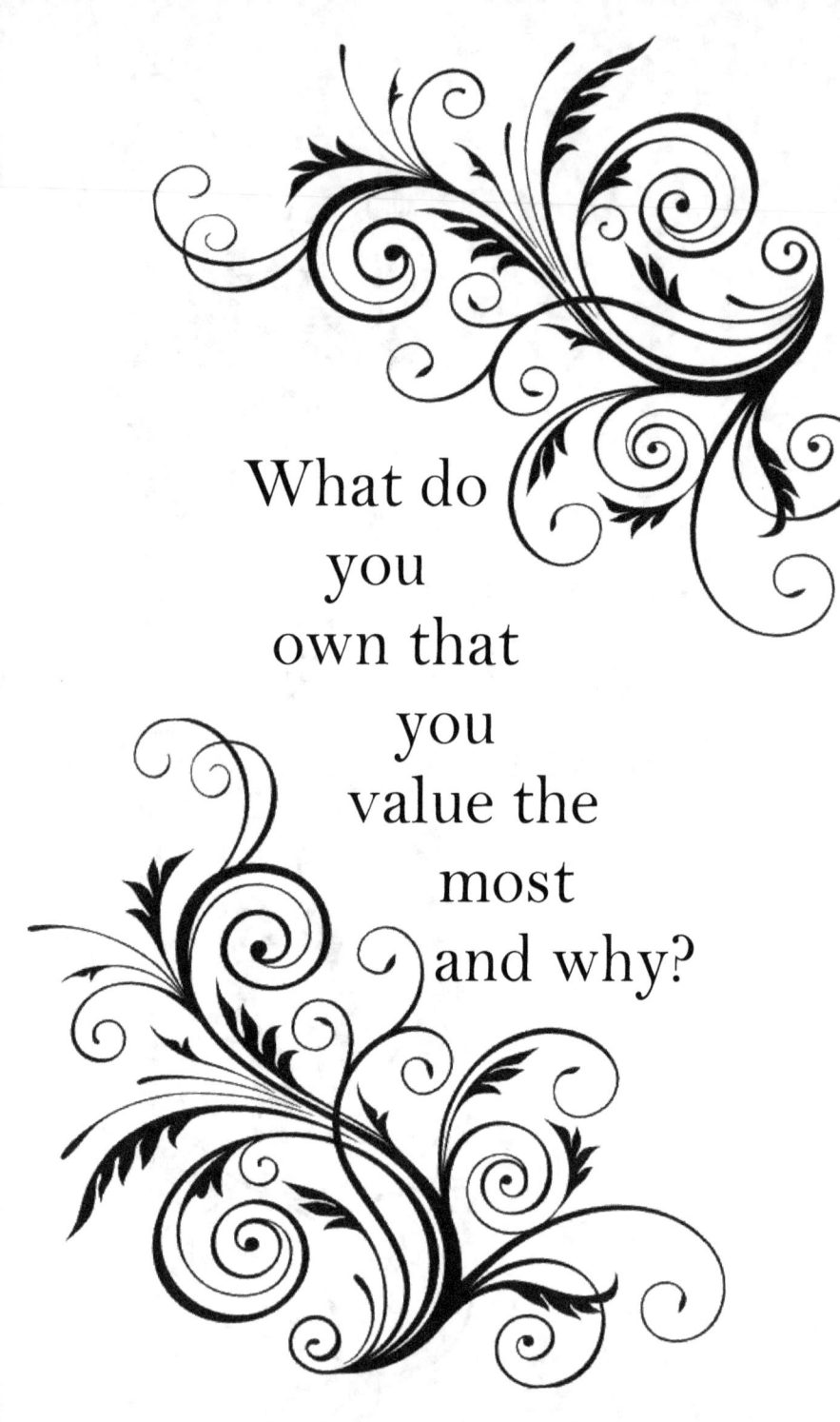

Talk about one project you want to complete in the next year.

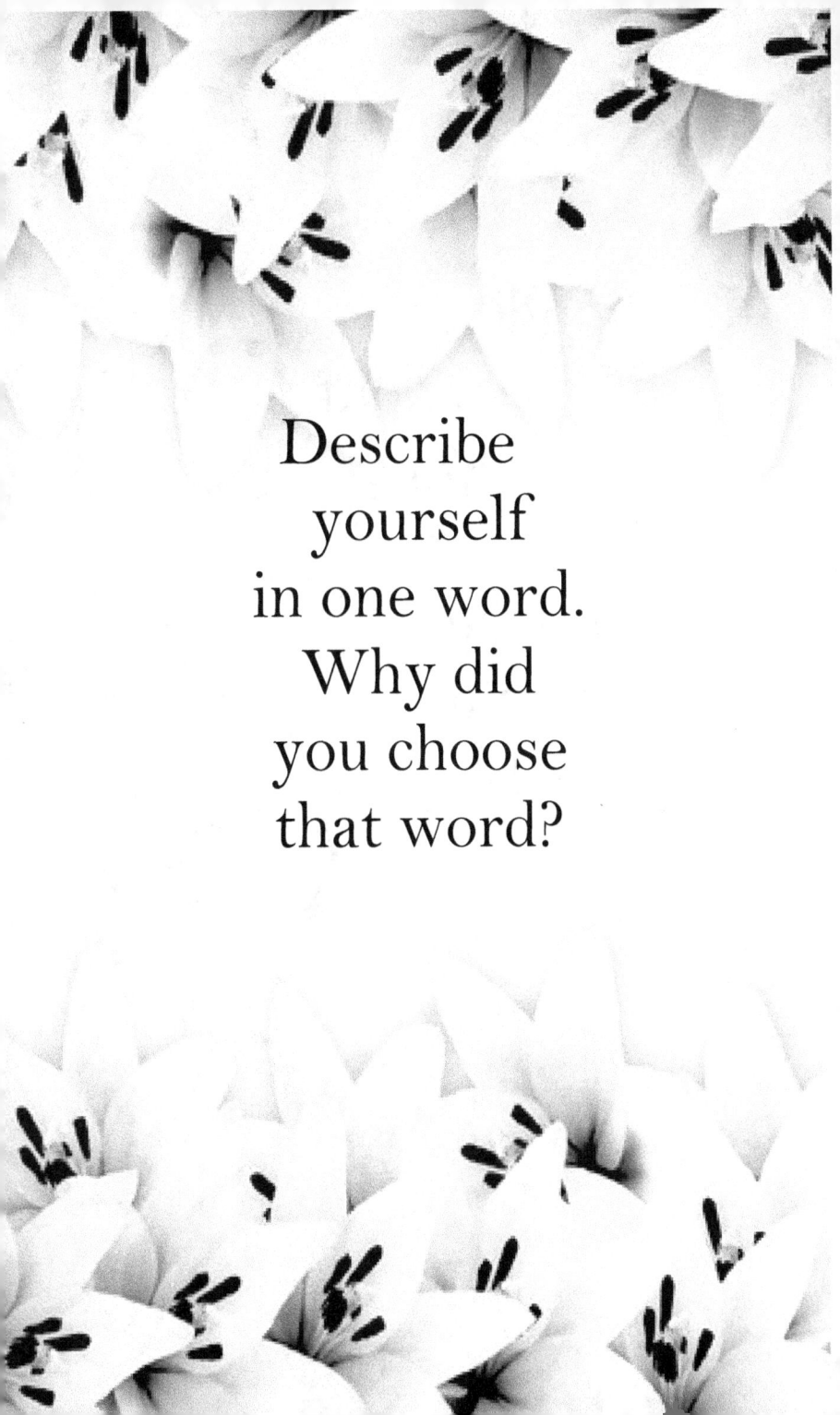

Describe yourself in one word. Why did you choose that word?

Cloud…
tell me about
a sad thing
that
happened
to you in
your life.

What are 3 things you love about yourself and why?

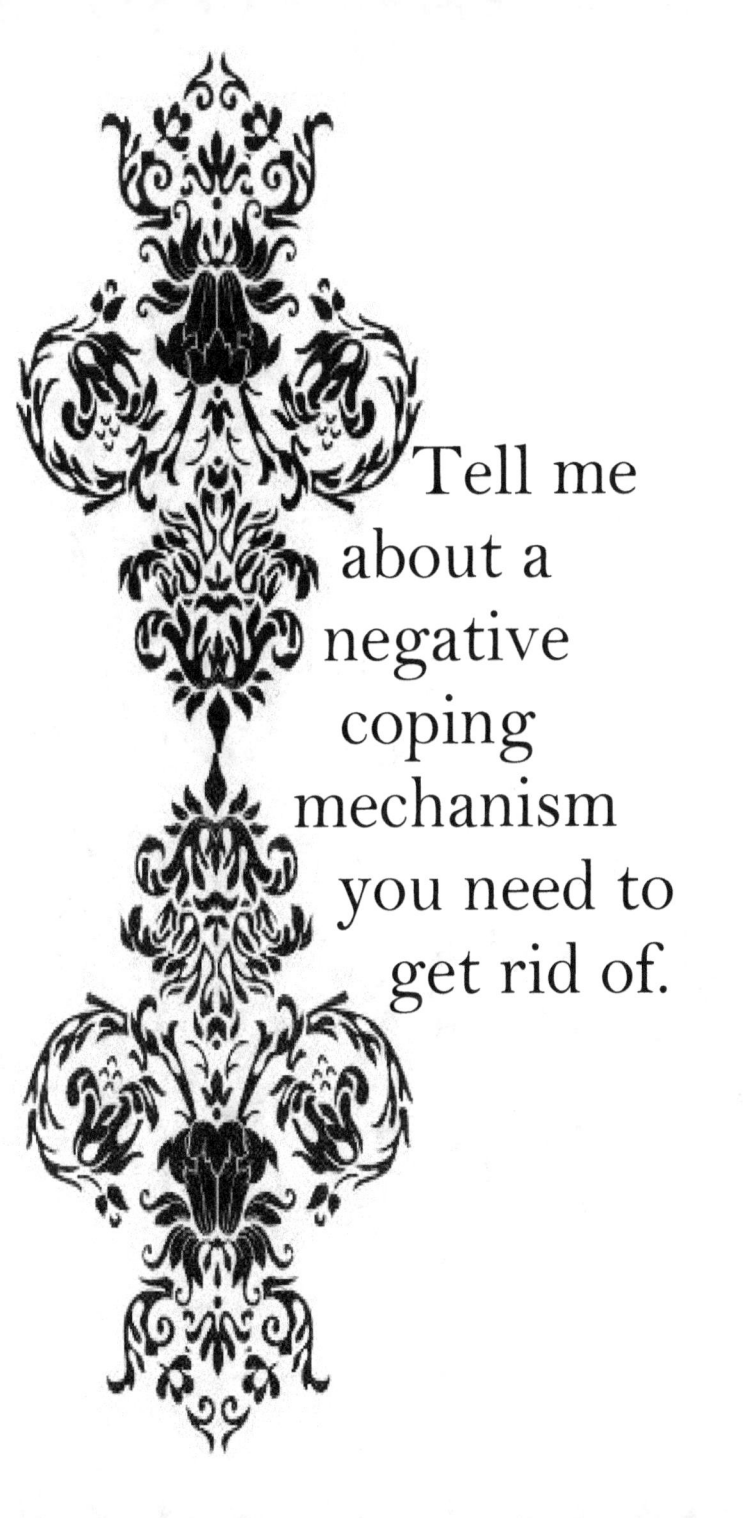

Describe yourself.

If someone asked you what you needed right now, what would you say?

When was the last time you felt sad? Tell me about it.

How did you feel about your father growing up?

Name something you want that you haven't asked God for yet.

Describe something that makes you smile.

Tell me about one of your most disturbing memories.

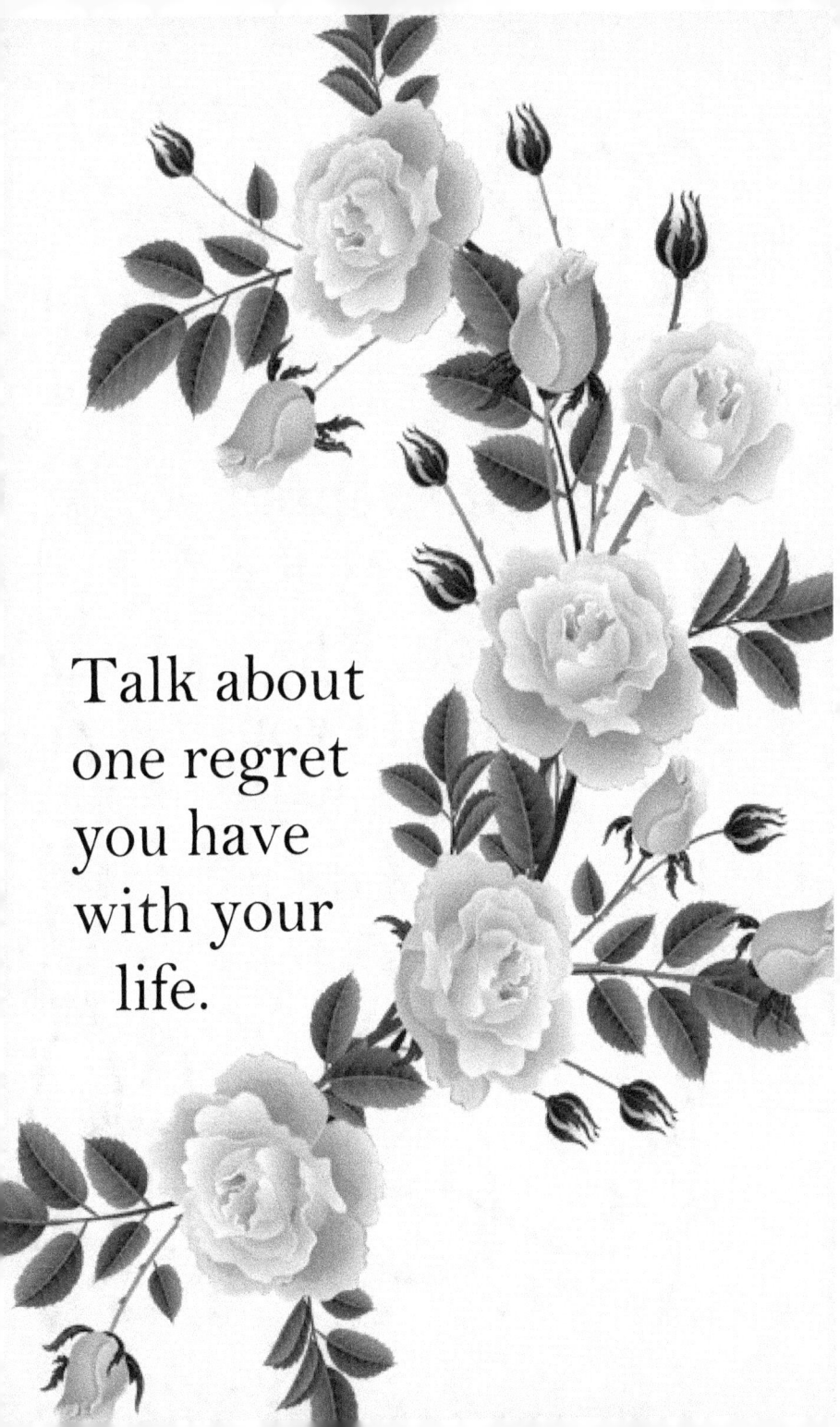
Talk about one regret you have with your life.

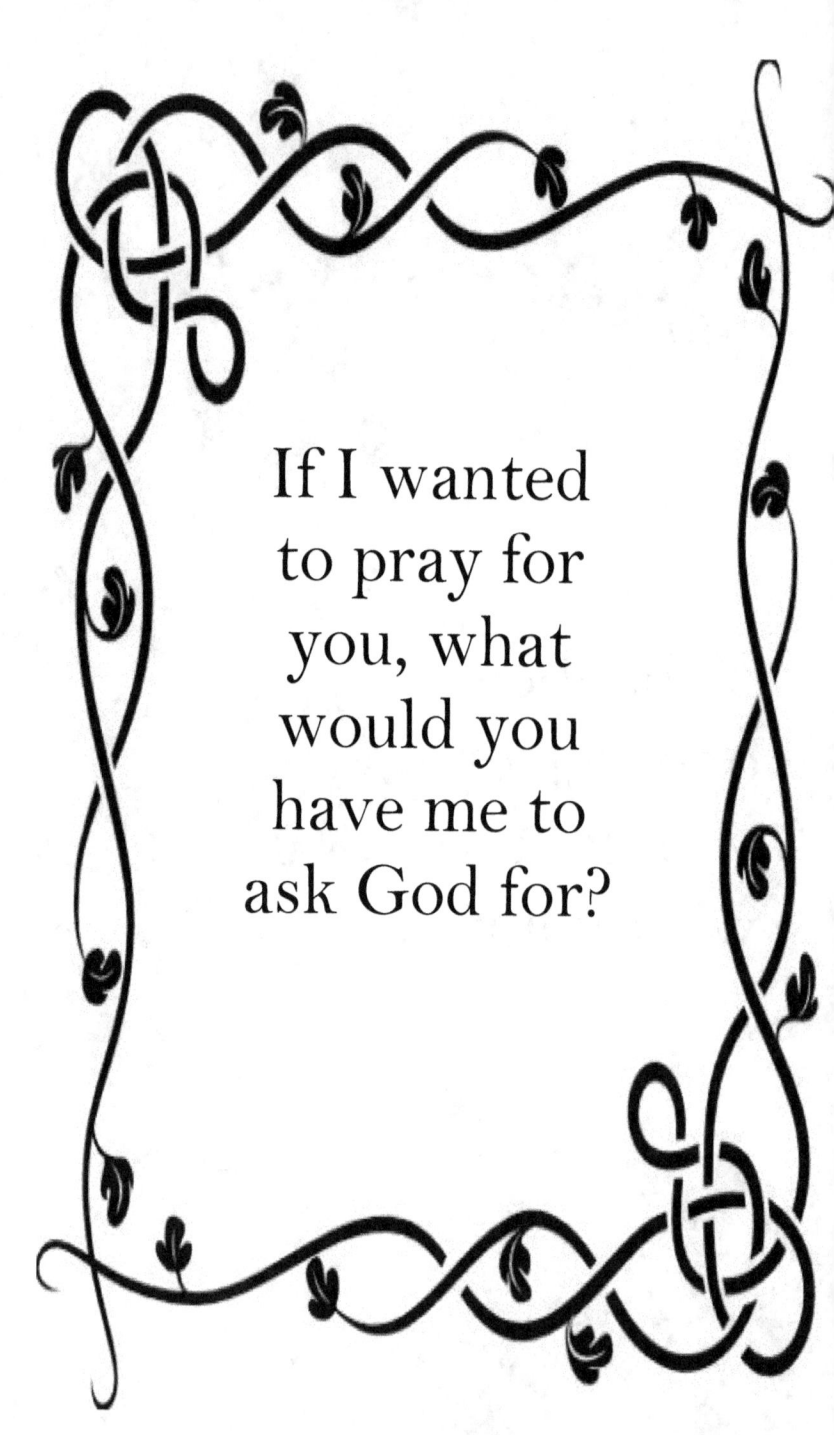

If I wanted to pray for you, what would you have me to ask God for?

Describe your dream career.

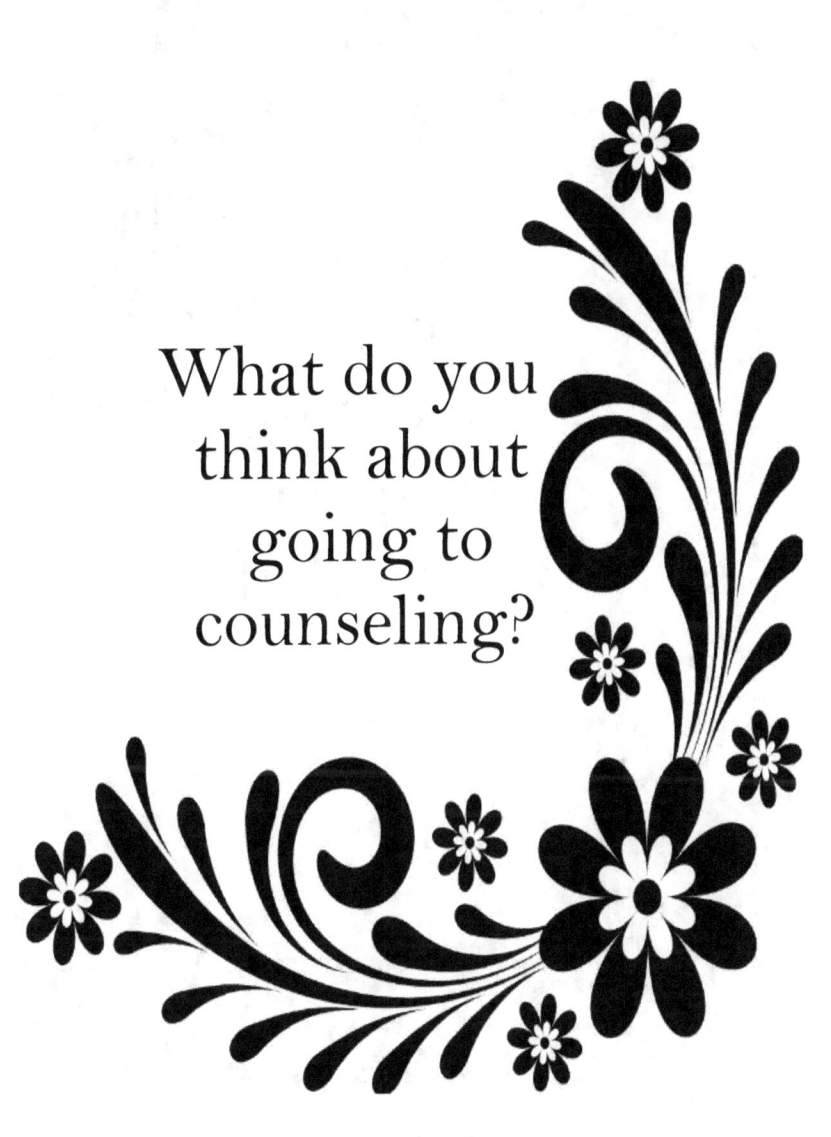

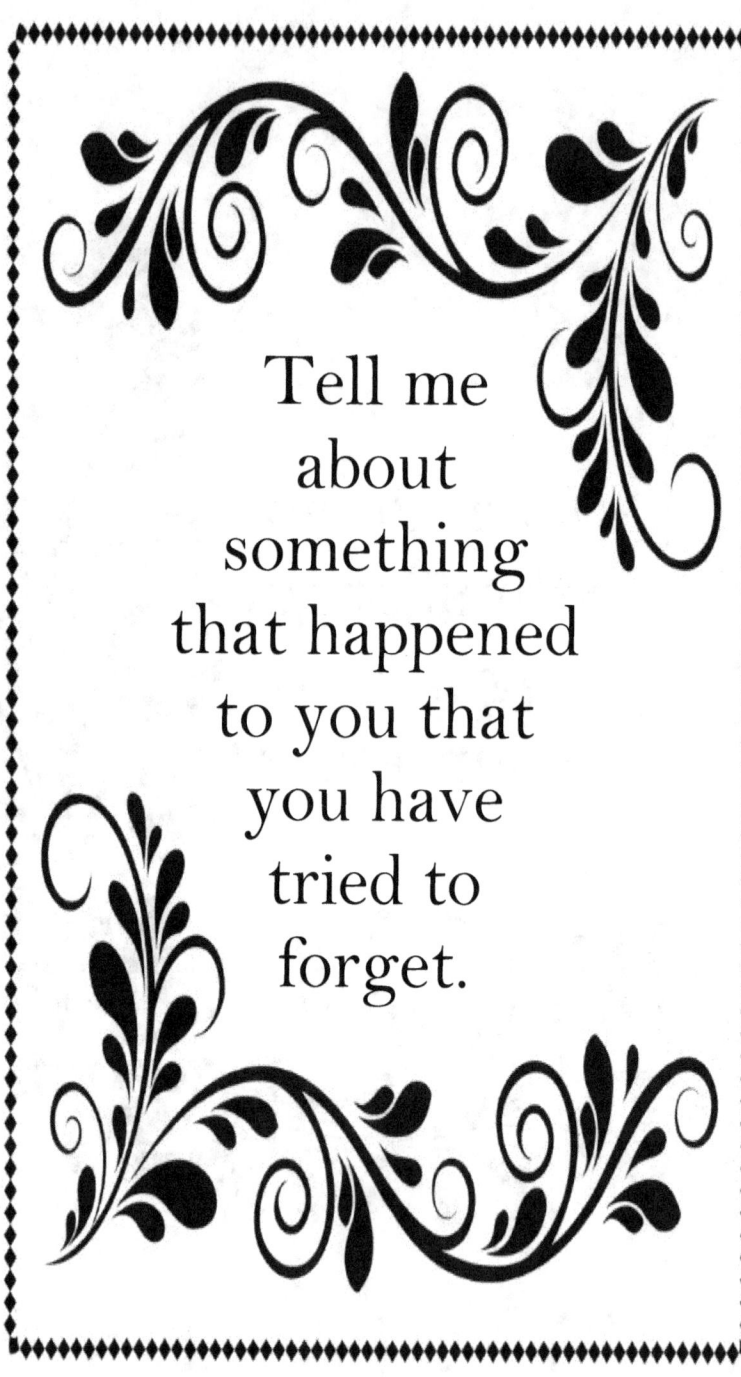

Tell me about something that happened to you that you have tried to forget.

When was the last time you said "I'm sorry" to someone? Tell me about it.

Tell me about a time when you felt scared.

Describe one nervous habit you have.

How would you describe the day you had today?

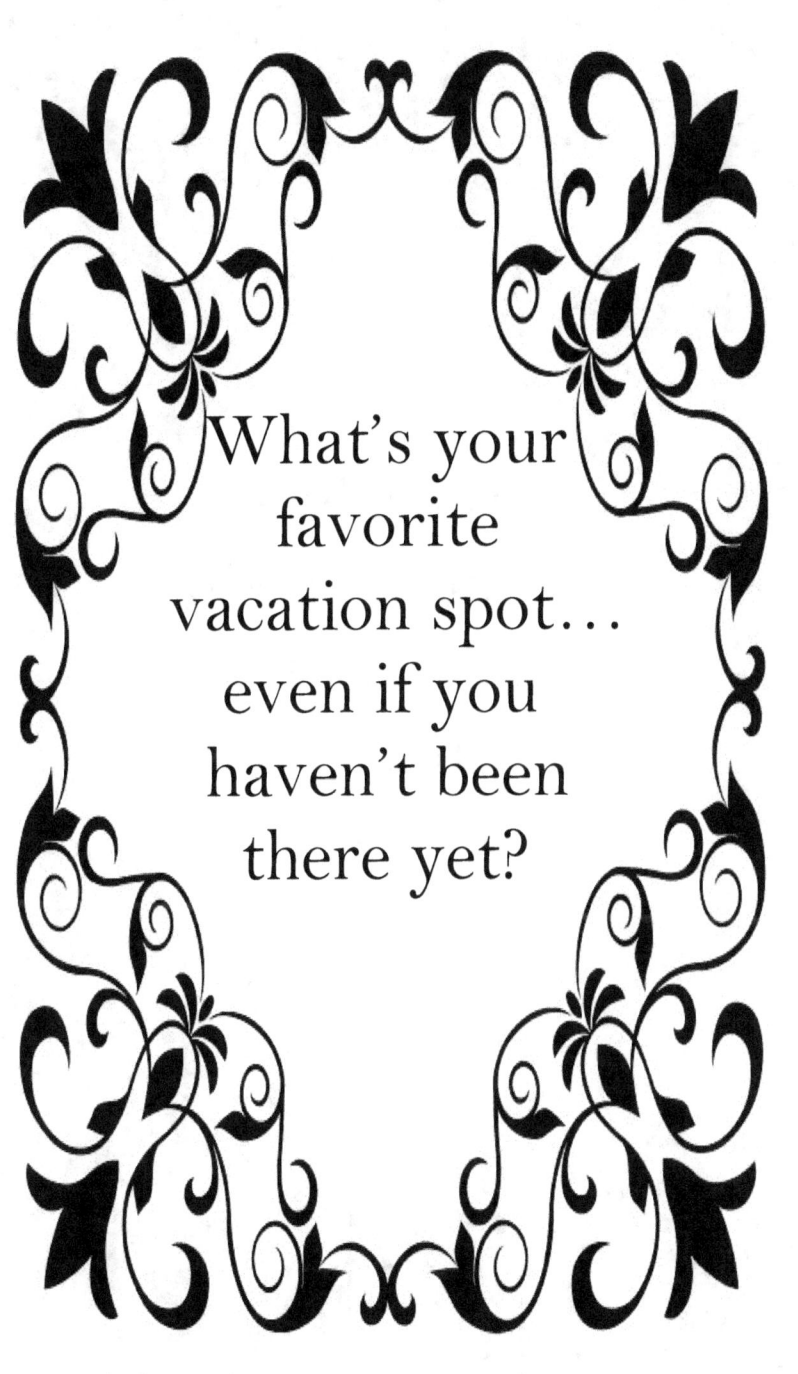

What's your favorite vacation spot… even if you haven't been there yet?

If there were no social media, how would you connect with people?

Name 2 of your favorite relatives. What makes them favorites?

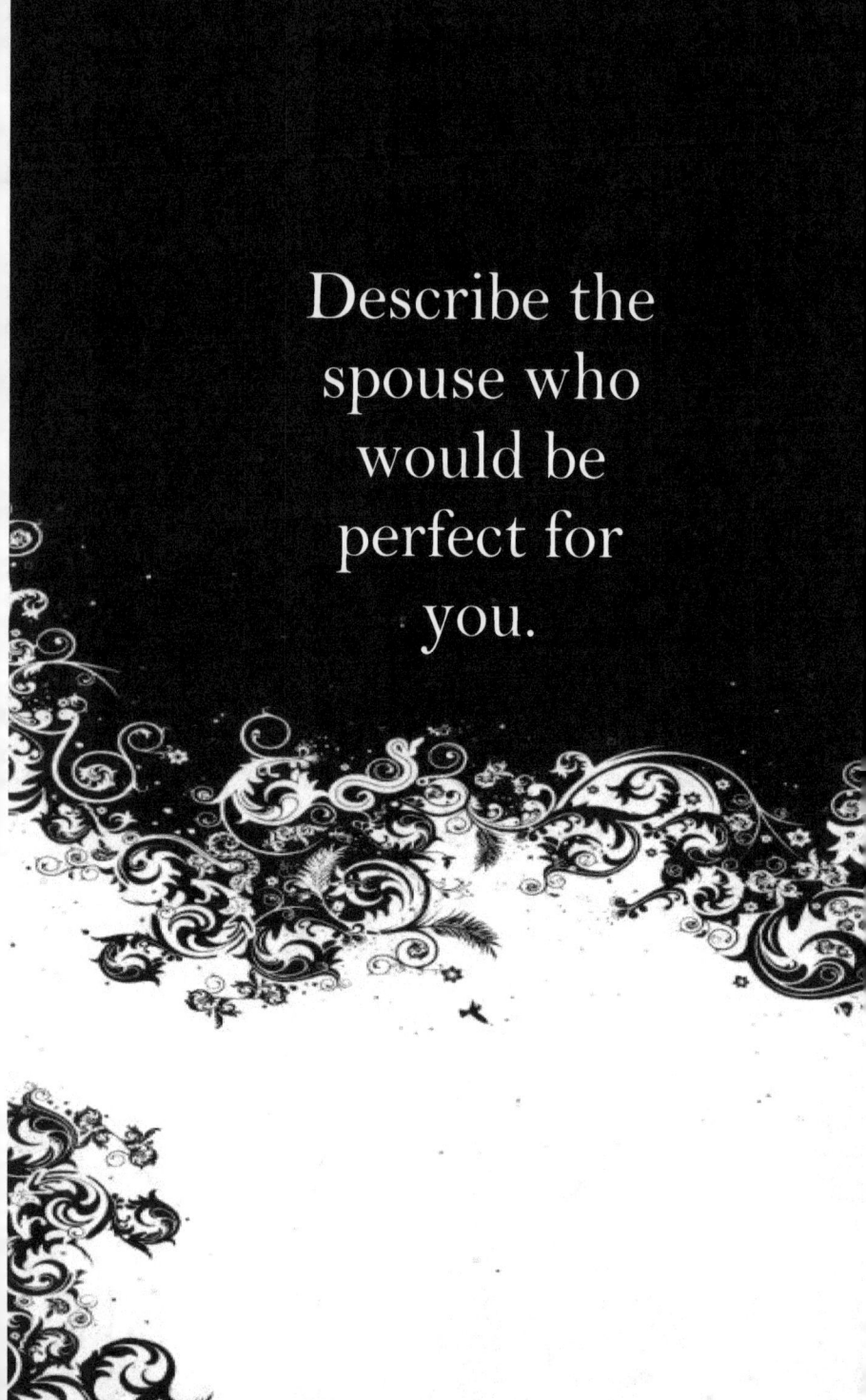

Describe the spouse who would be perfect for you.

What will you do with your journal once it's full?

If you could ask one of your parents anything, what would it be?

When was the last time someone surprised you? Tell me about it.

What do you enjoy doing in your alone time?

Describe your dream vacation.

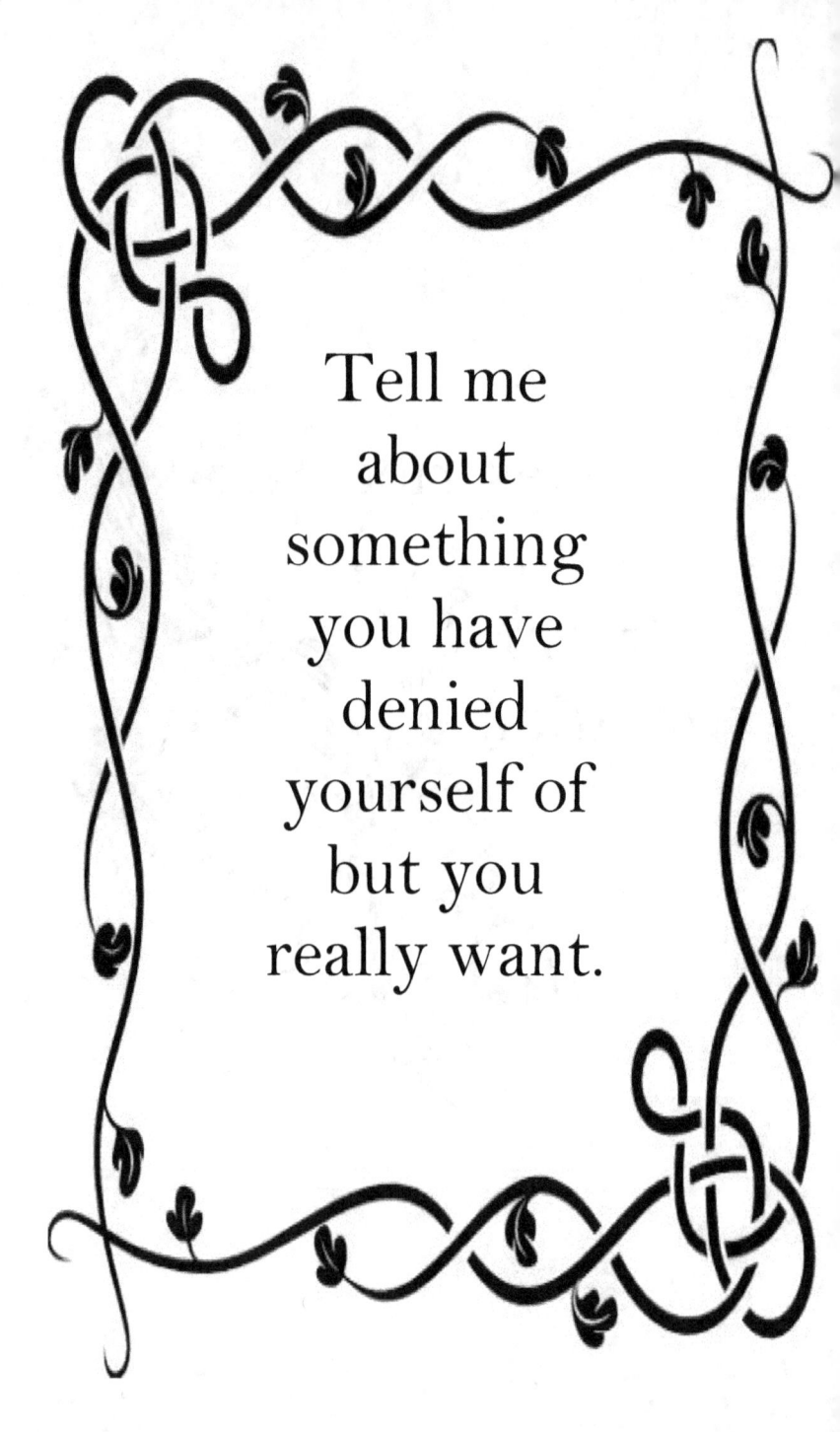

What's your favorite meal and when was the last time you had it?

Talk about a time when you overreacted to a comment.

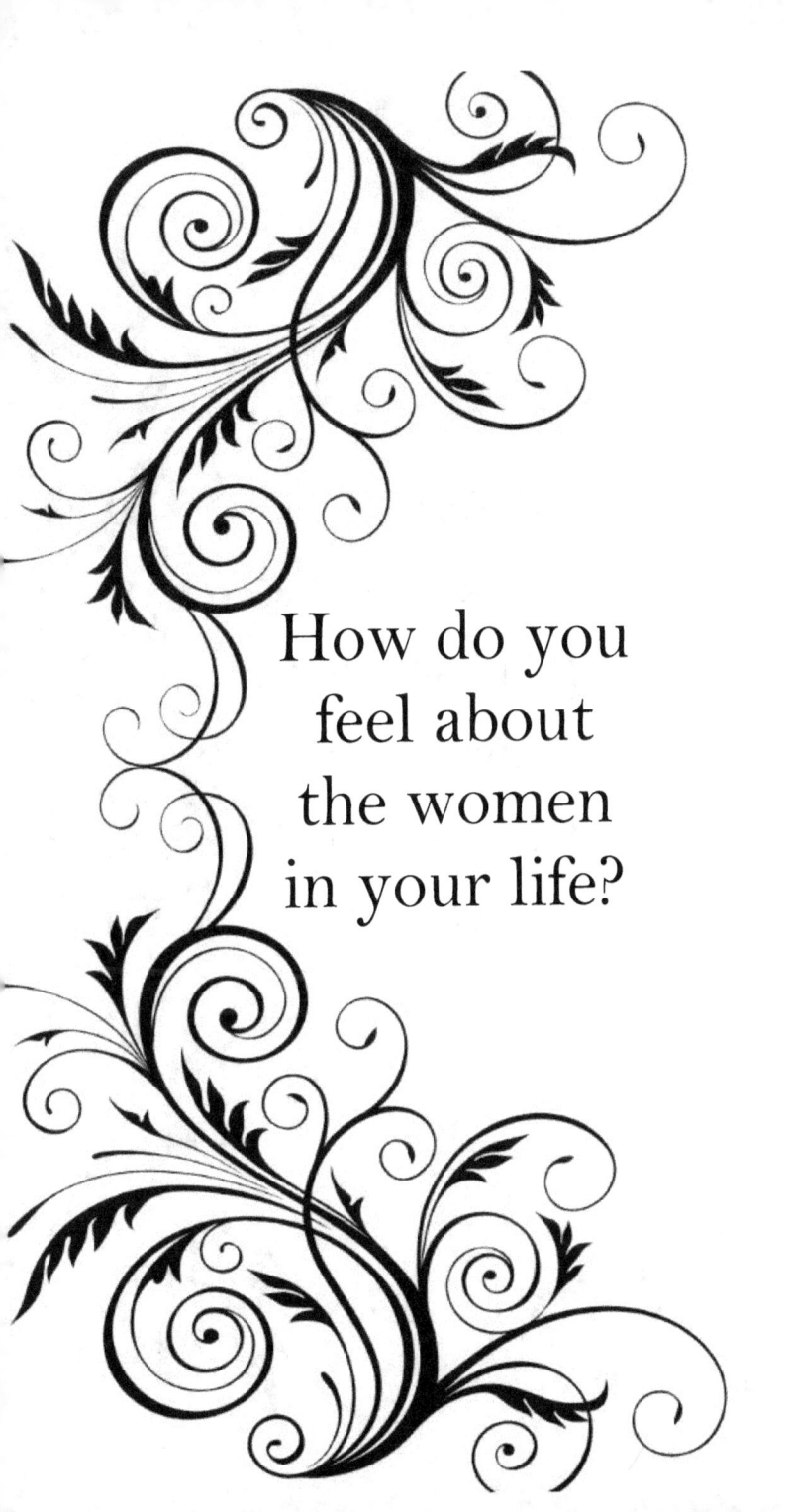

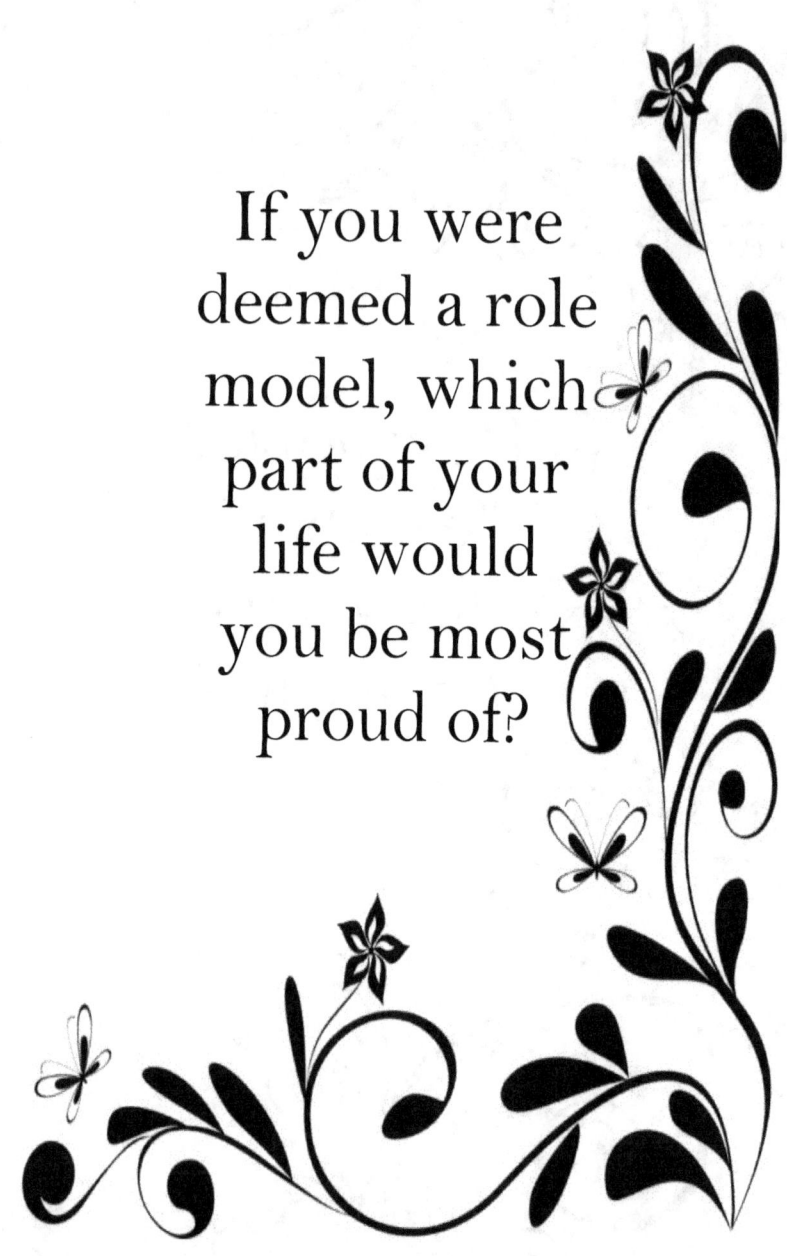

If you were deemed a role model, which part of your life would you be most proud of?

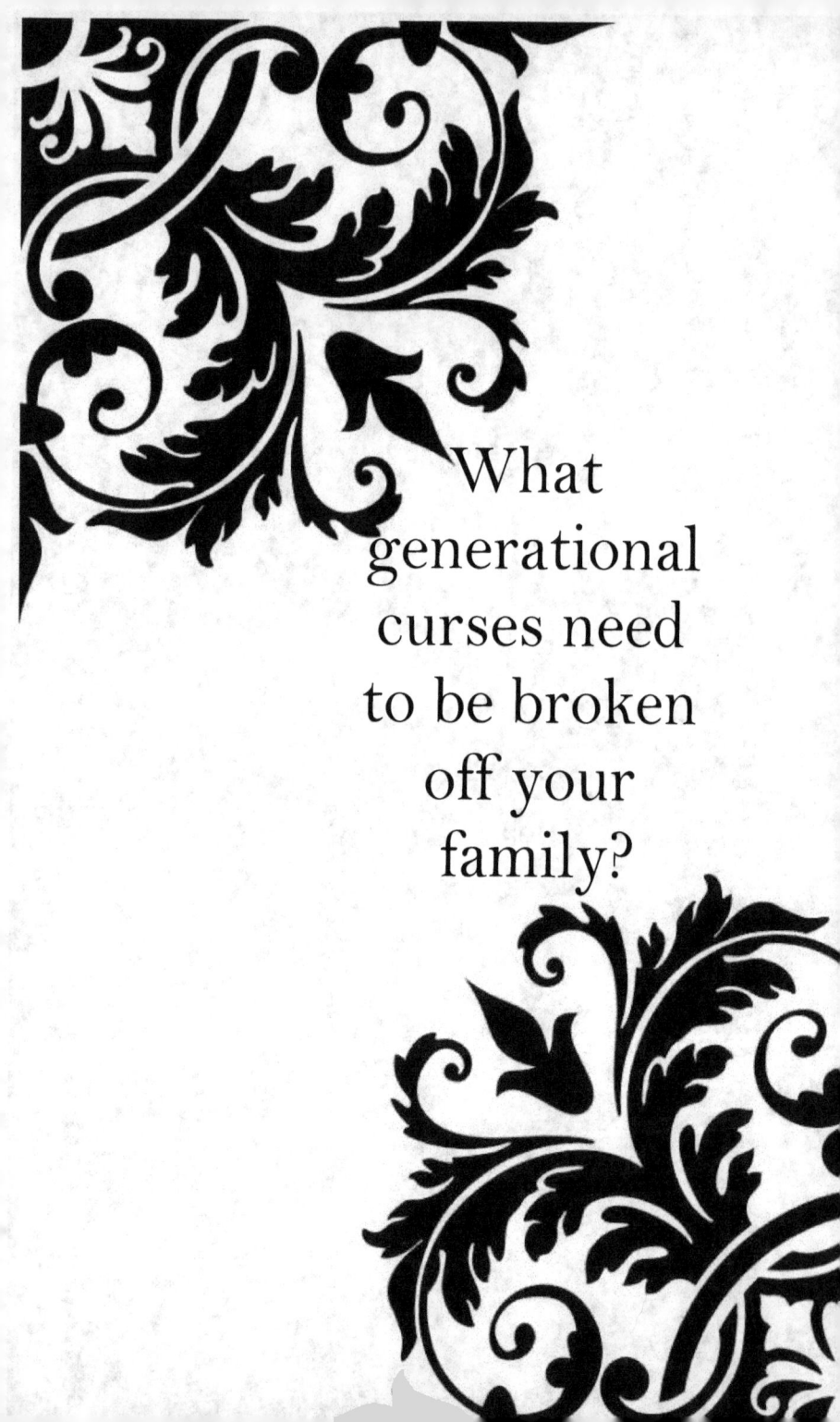
What generational curses need to be broken off your family?

Describe a time when you wanted to stand up for yourself but didn't.

Talk about a time when you asked for help.

When was the last time you felt mad? Tell me about it.

Tell me one thing that worries you about the future.

What would make your life complete?

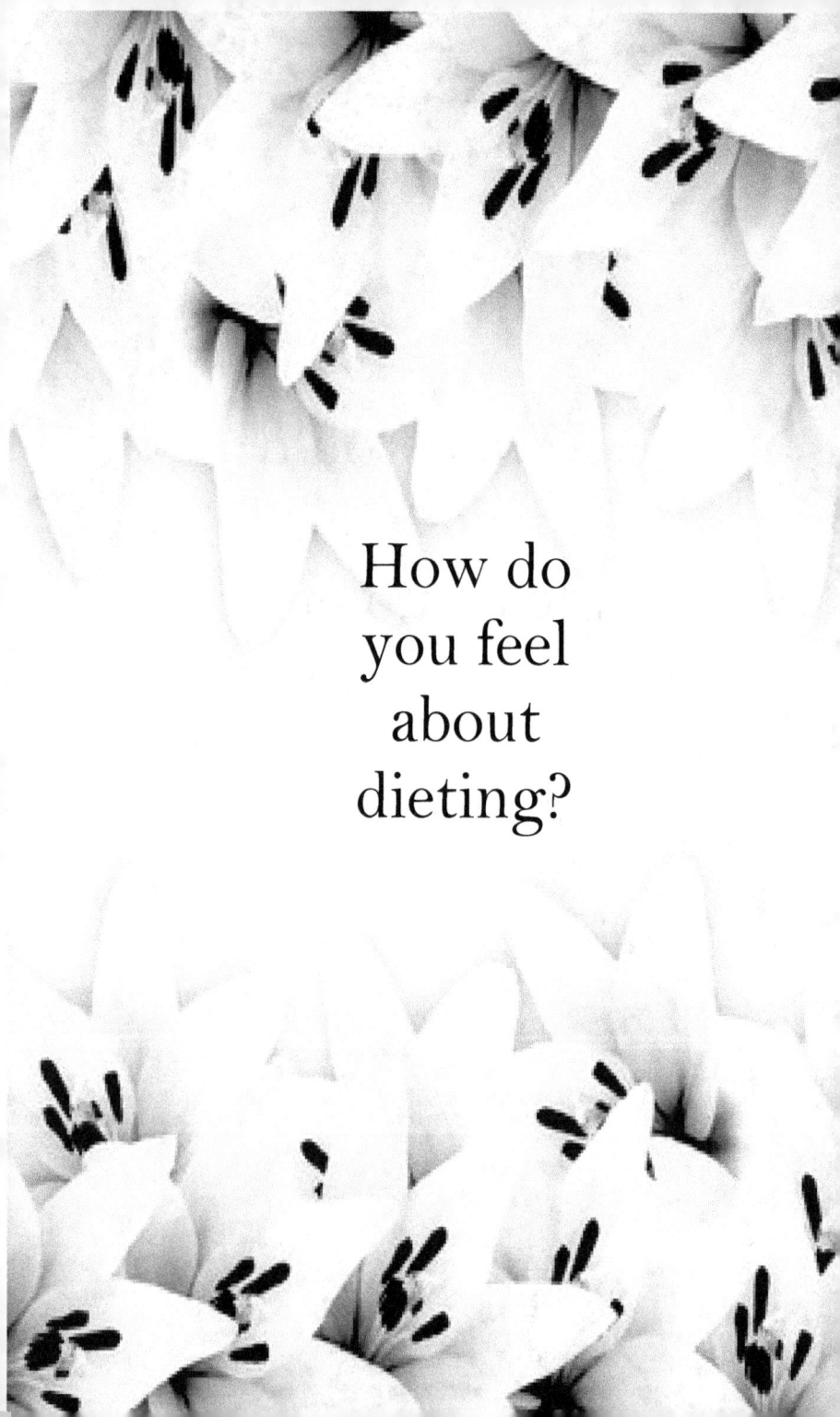

How do you feel about dieting?

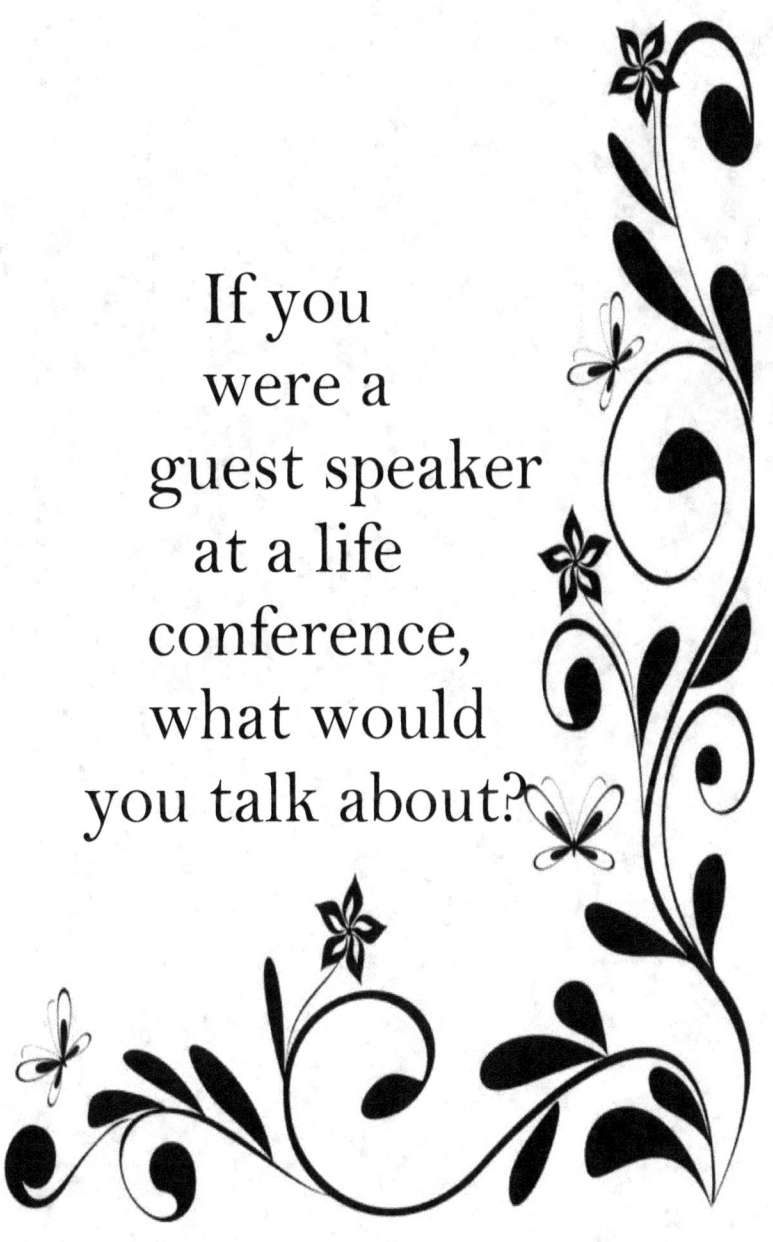

If you were a guest speaker at a life conference, what would you talk about?

Describe your idea of quality time with a loved one.

Would you consider yourself a people pleaser? Why or why not?

Tell me about a time when you felt unappreciated.

Talk about something in your life you have given up on.

What tv, movie or book character do you most identify with and why?

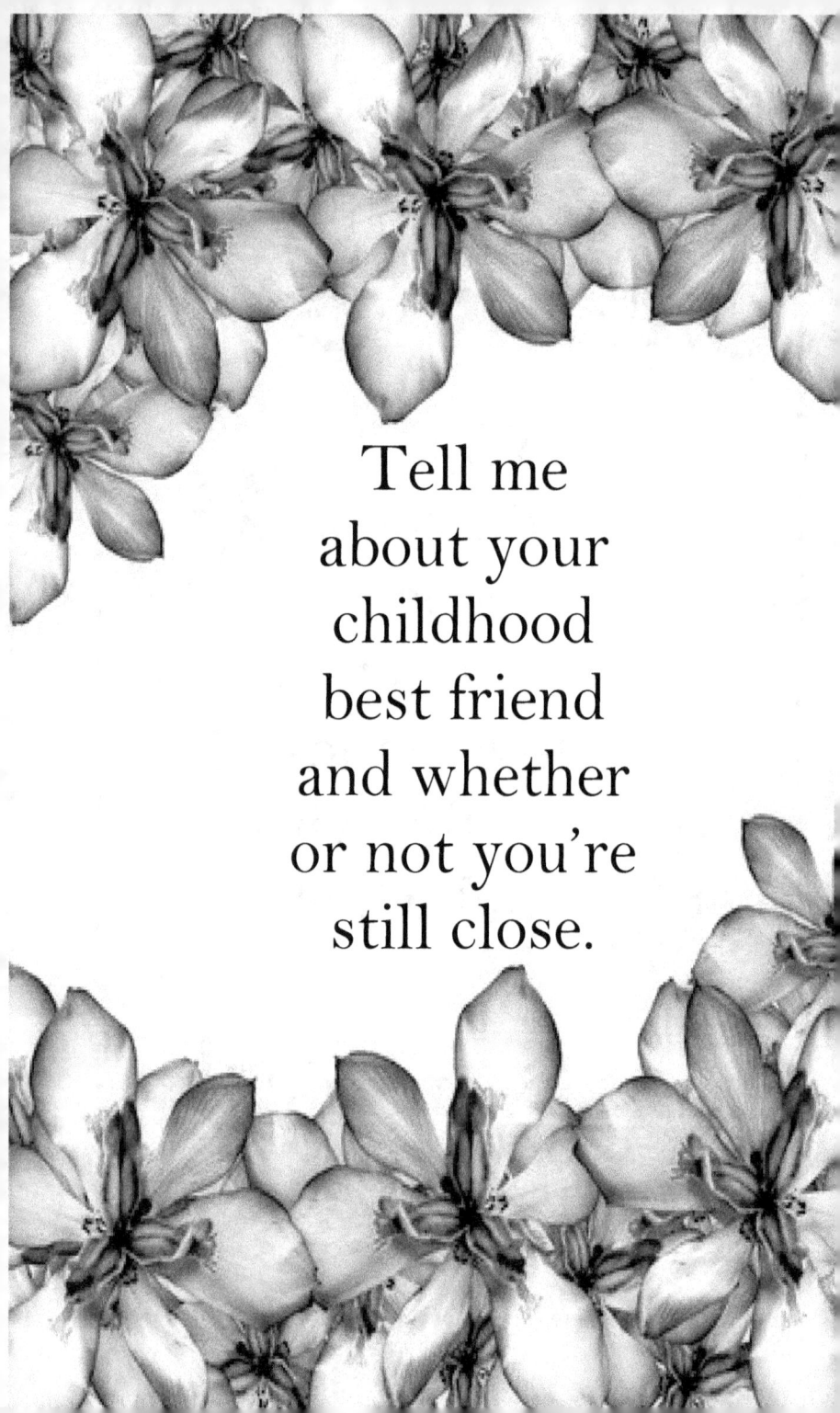

Tell me about your childhood best friend and whether or not you're still close.

Describe a situation where you needed to say "no" but didn't.

What activities in your life make you feel purposeful?

How well
do you sleep?
Why?

Talk about one thing you have not resolved from the past.

When was the last time someone hurt you? Tell me about it.

Describe your childhood.

What
do
you
think
about
yourself?

Do you prefer texting, talking, or social media? Why?

Tell me about a movie you love and why you love it.

If you were required to entertain a large crowd what would you do?

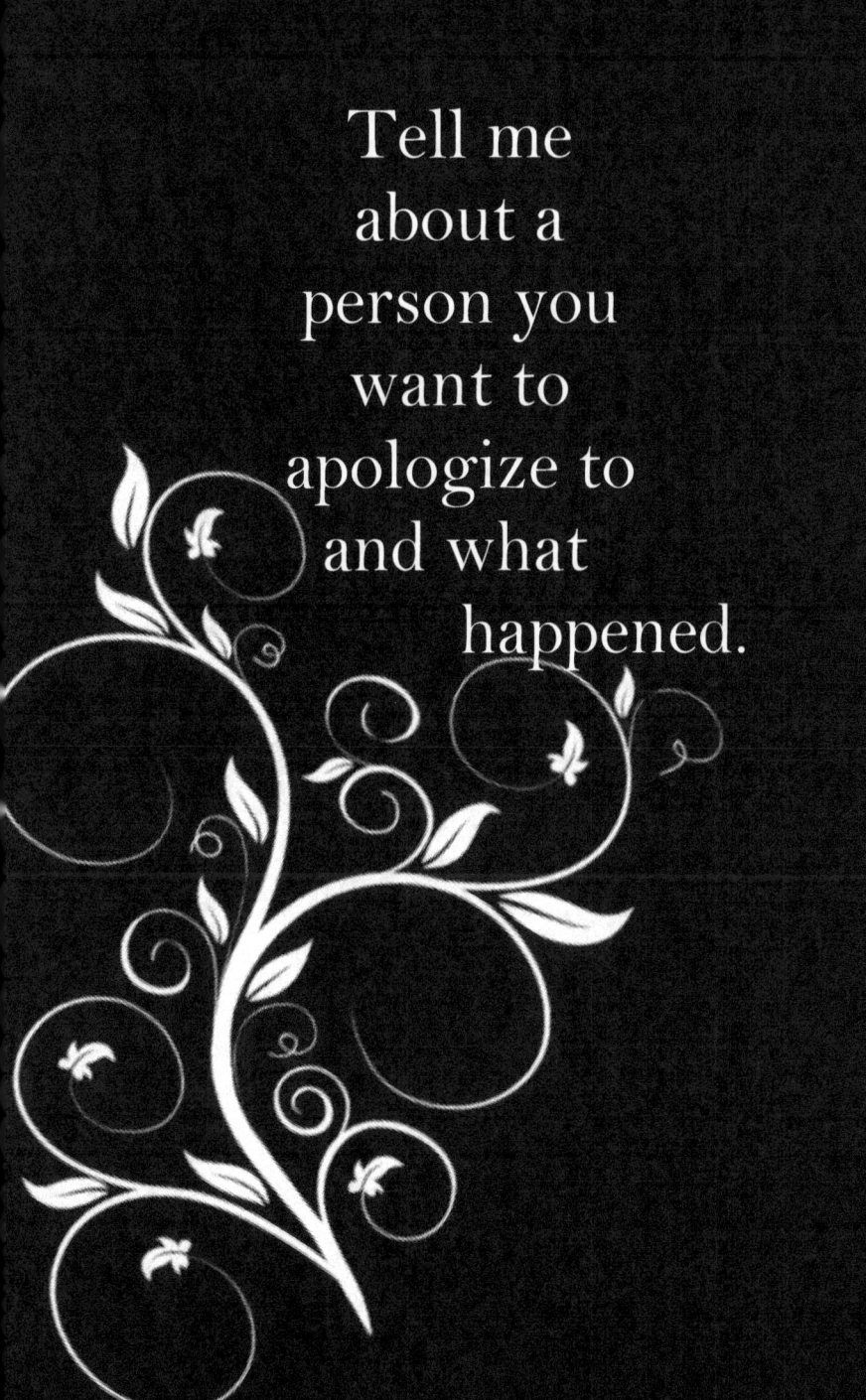

Tell me about a time where you felt loved.

Describe a time when you felt you were taken advantage of.

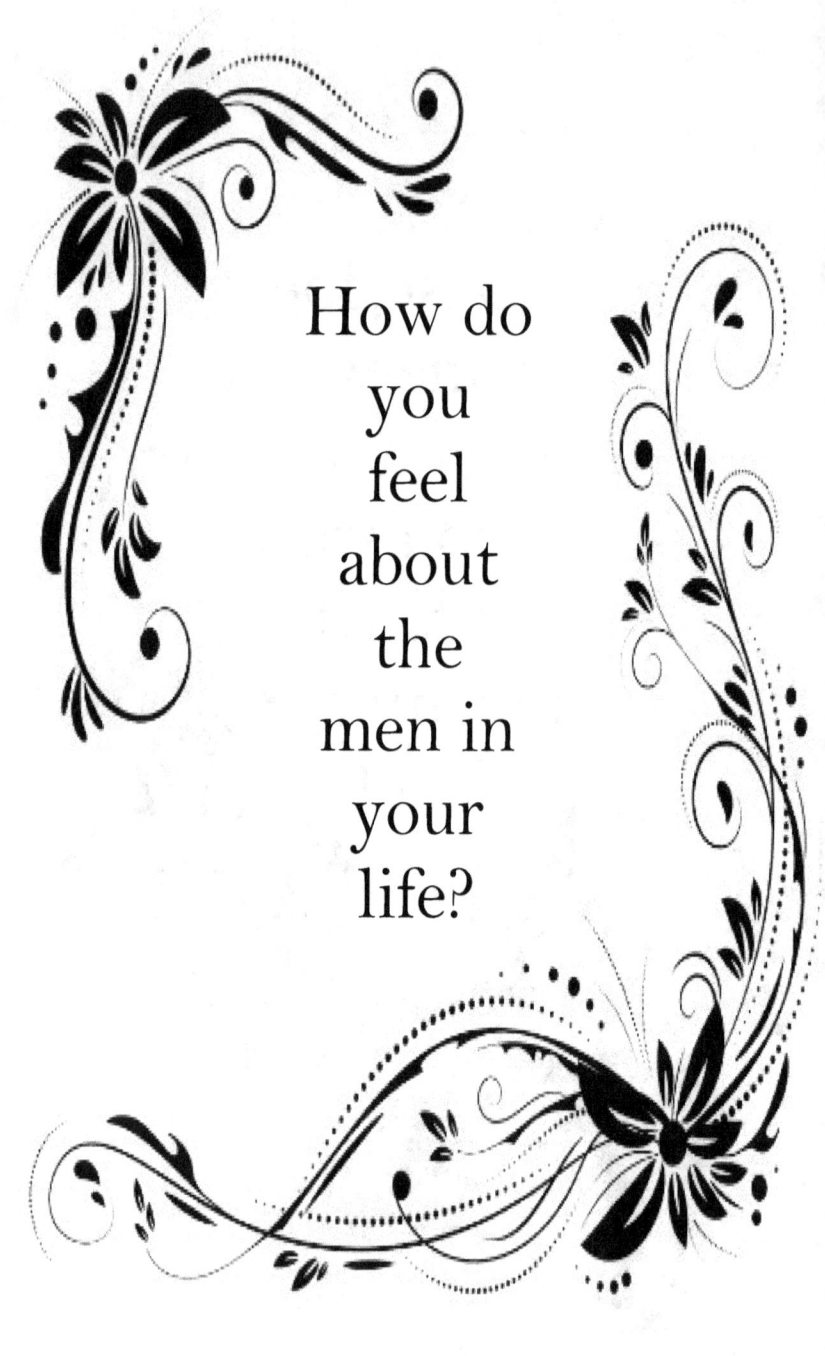

How do you feel about the men in your life?

What part of your life still brings you shame?

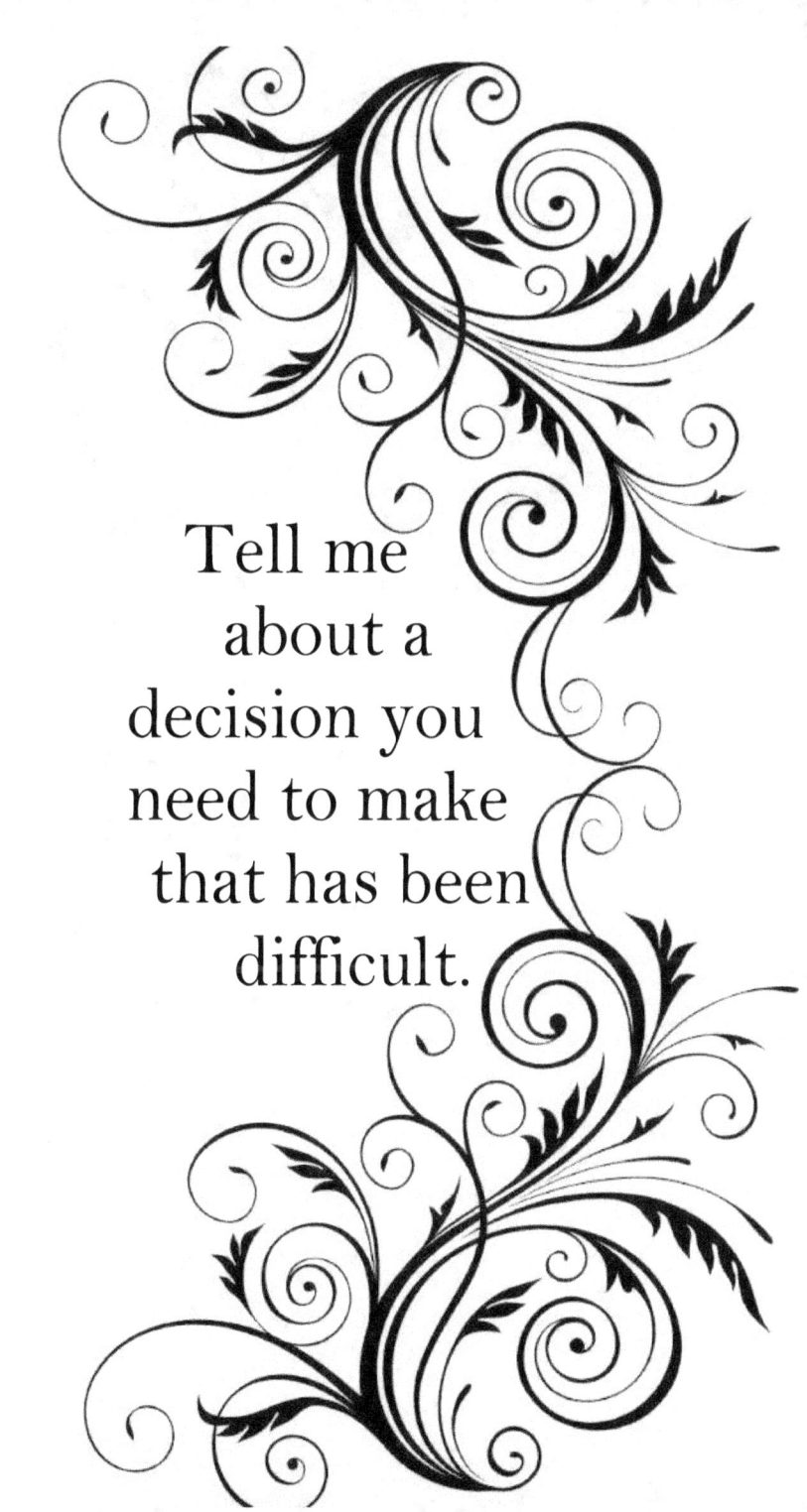

Tell me about a decision you need to make that has been difficult.

Describe 2 things that are keeping you stuck.

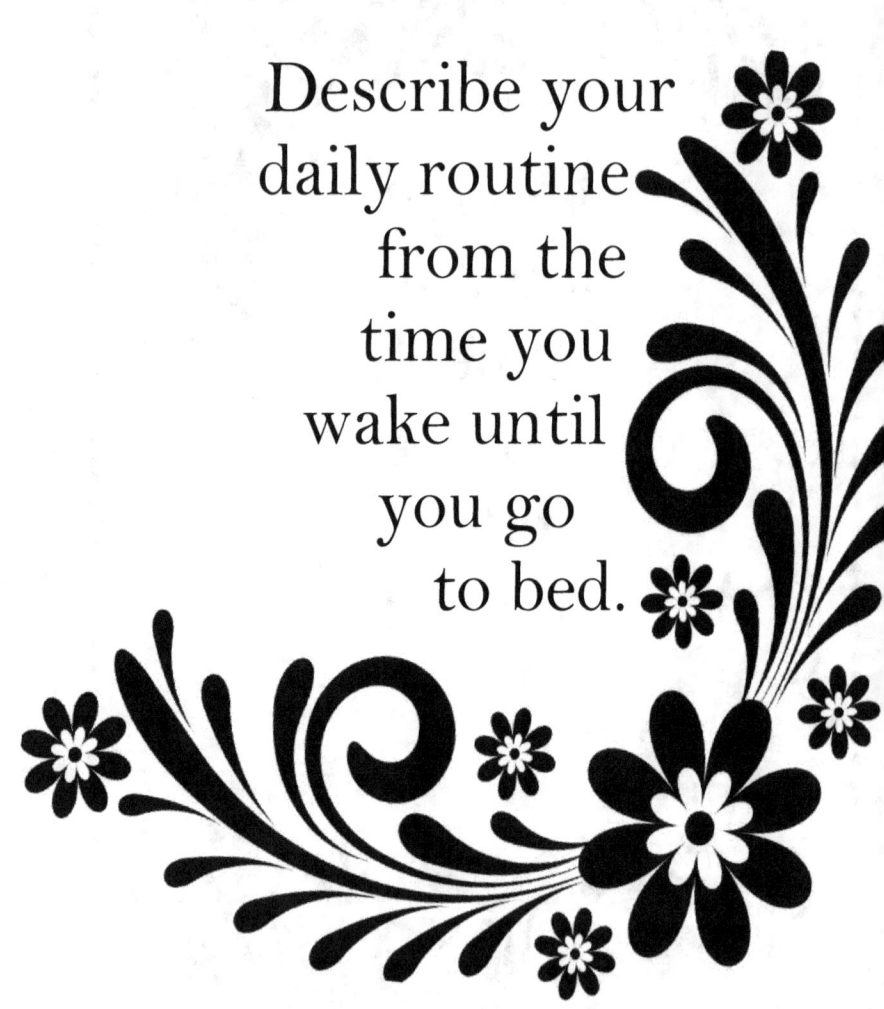

When was the last time you felt brave? Tell me about it.

What were you thinking about right before you picked up your journal?

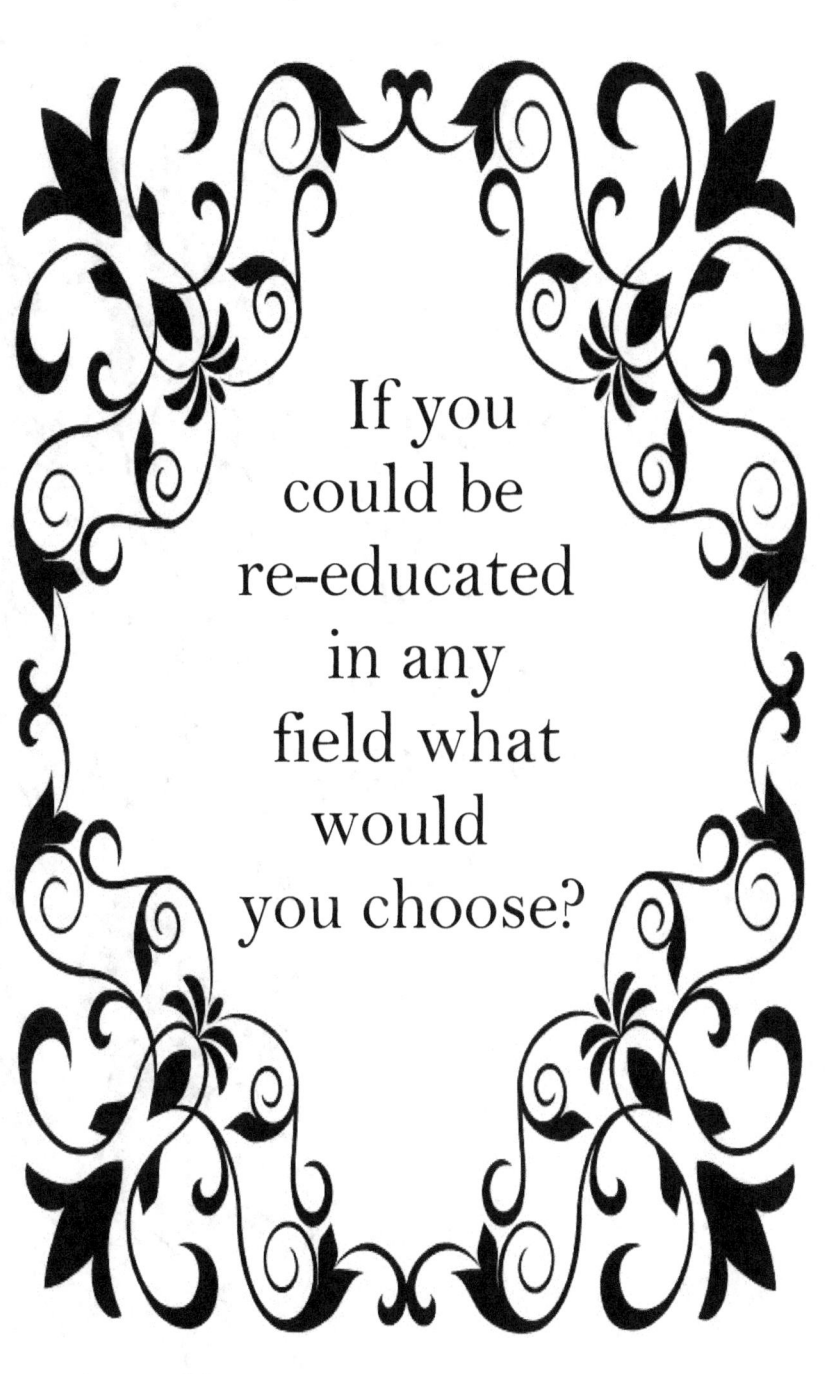

What is your least favorite food and why?

Once
you have
accomplished
all your
dreams
what will
your life
look like?

When was the last time you felt embarrassed? Tell me about it.

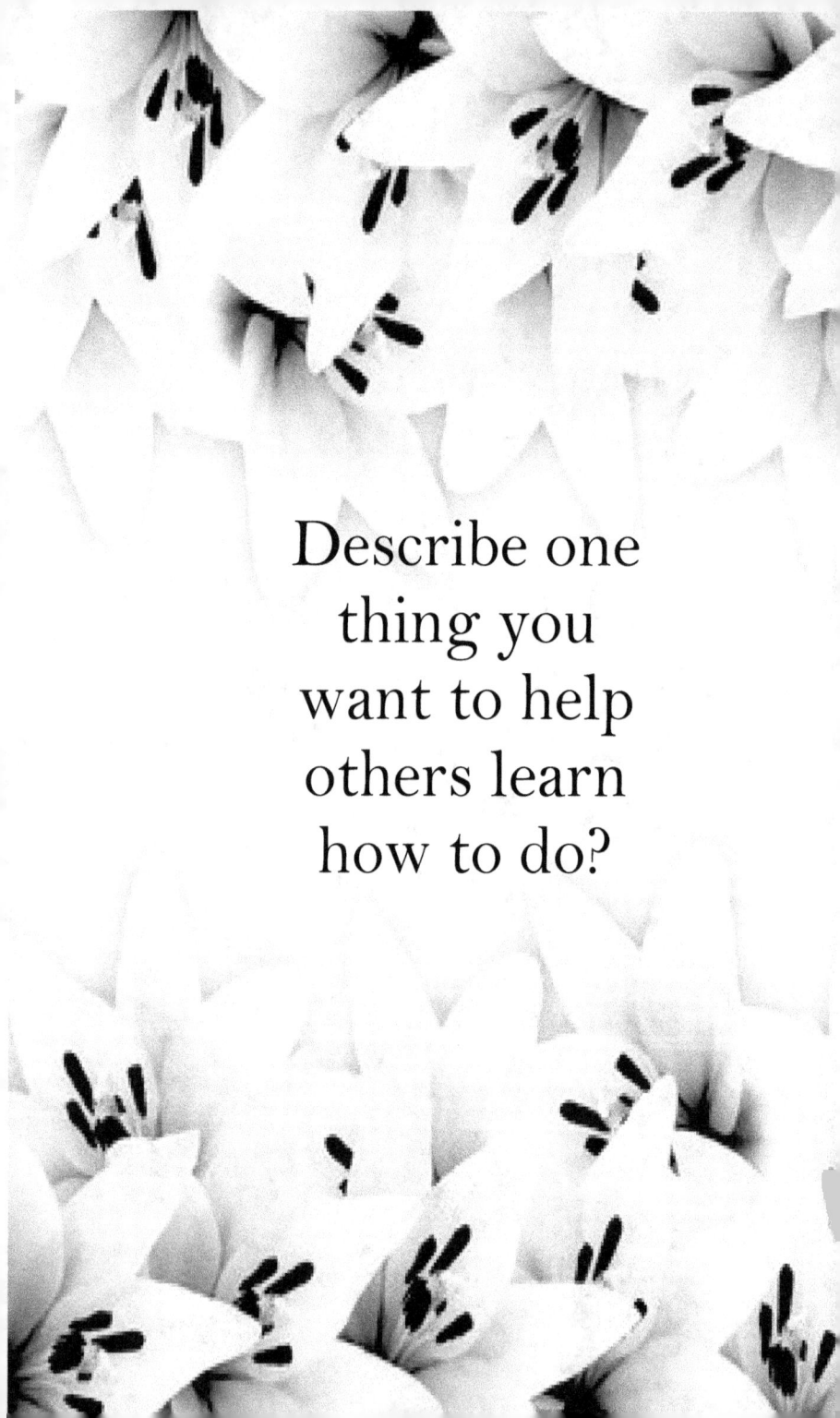

Describe one thing you want to help others learn how to do?

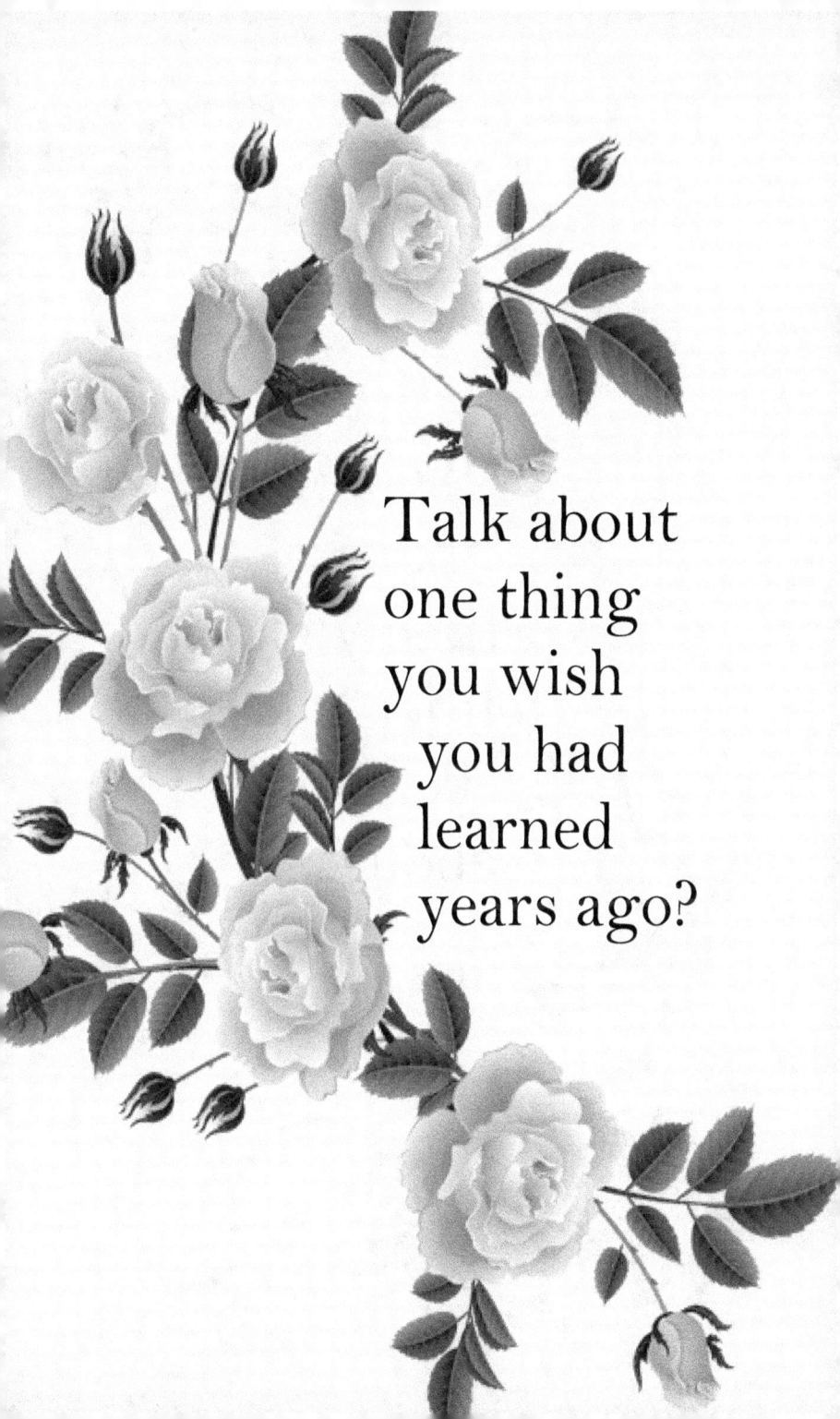

Talk about one thing you wish you had learned years ago?

When was the last time you felt jealous? Tell me about it.

What were you doing right before you picked up your journal?

Describe the best date you ever took yourself on… even if you haven't gone yet.

Who is your favorite actor/actress and why?

If God allowed
you to see
one thing in
the future
what would
you want
to see?

If you could bring back any family member who would it be and why?

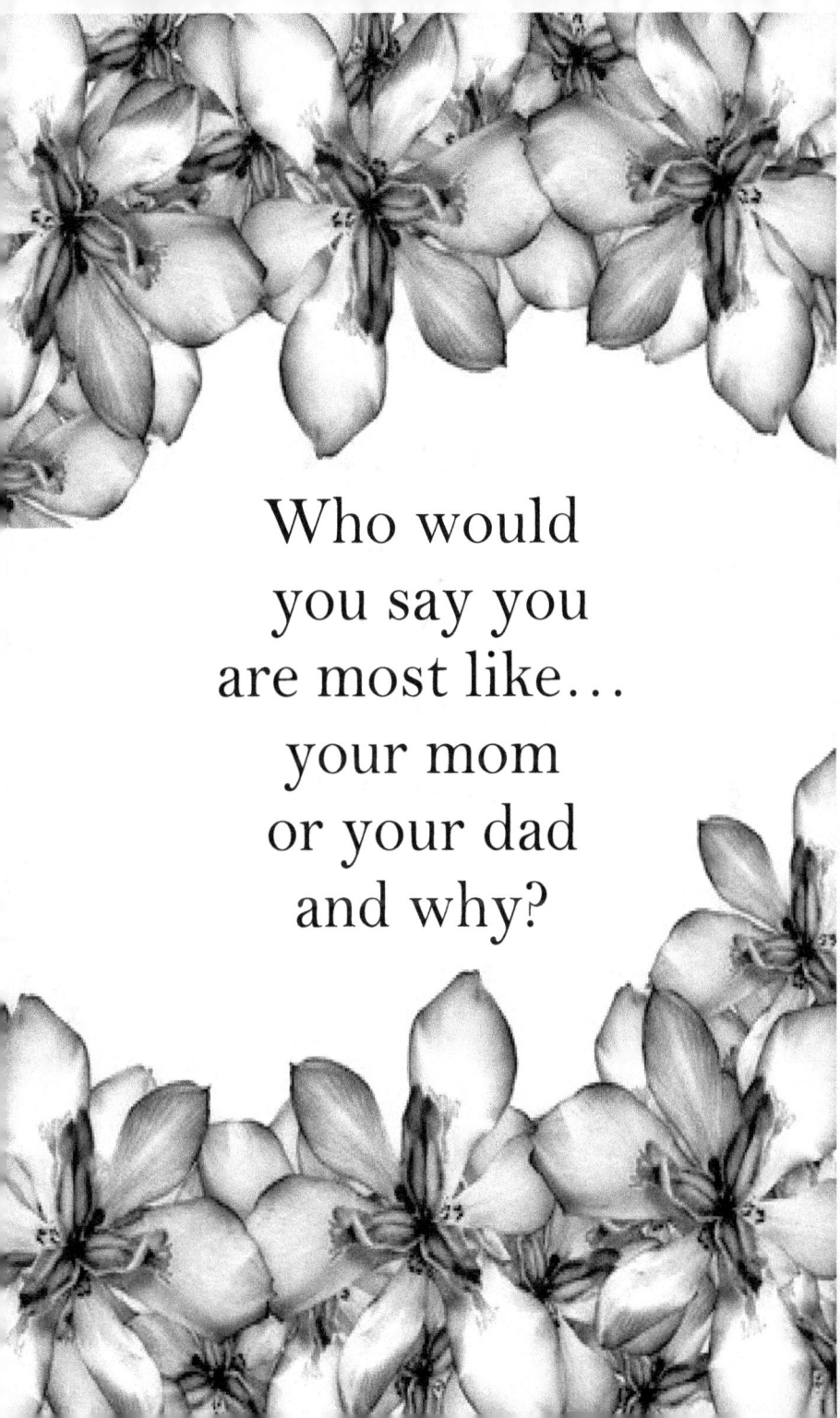

Who would you say you are most like… your mom or your dad and why?

What is your favorite color and why?

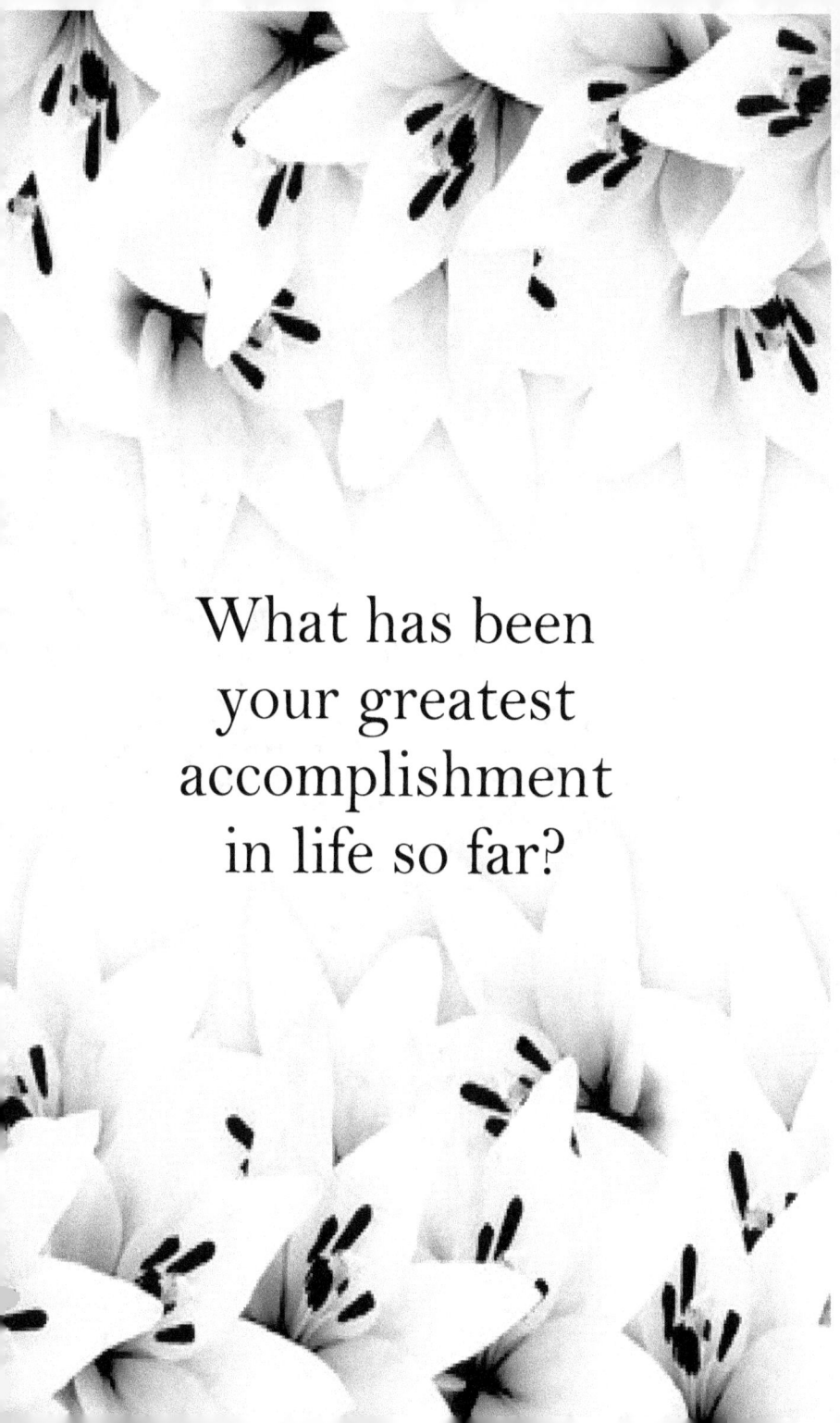

Do you consider yourself a strong person? Why or Why not?

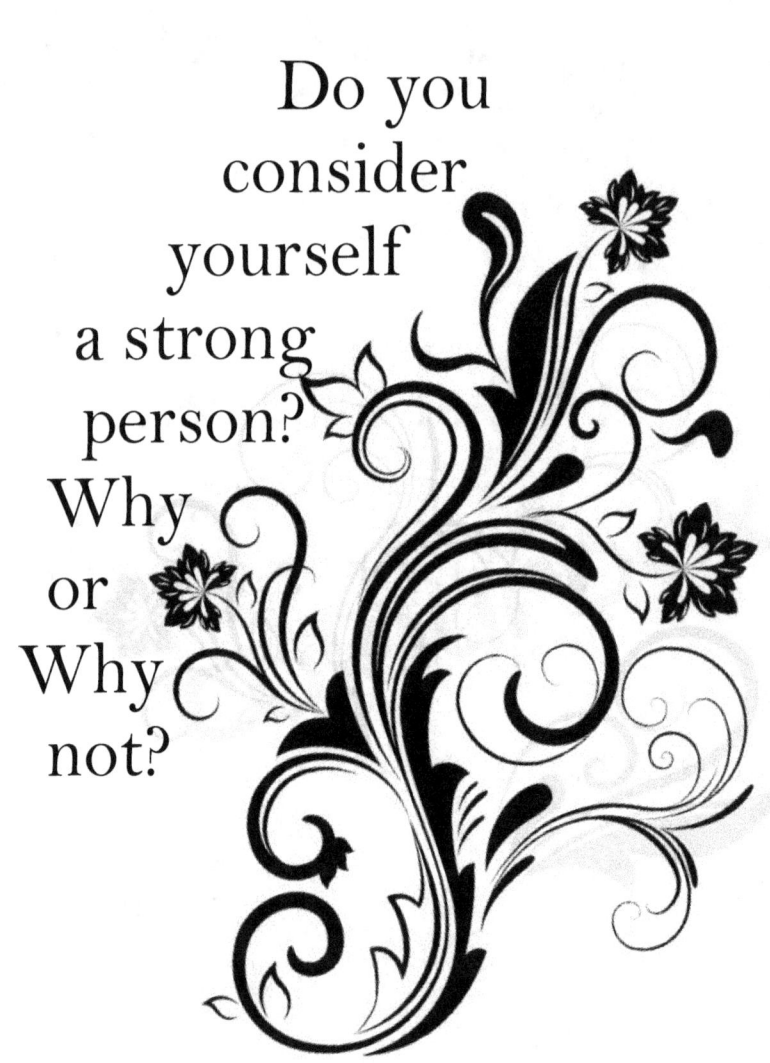

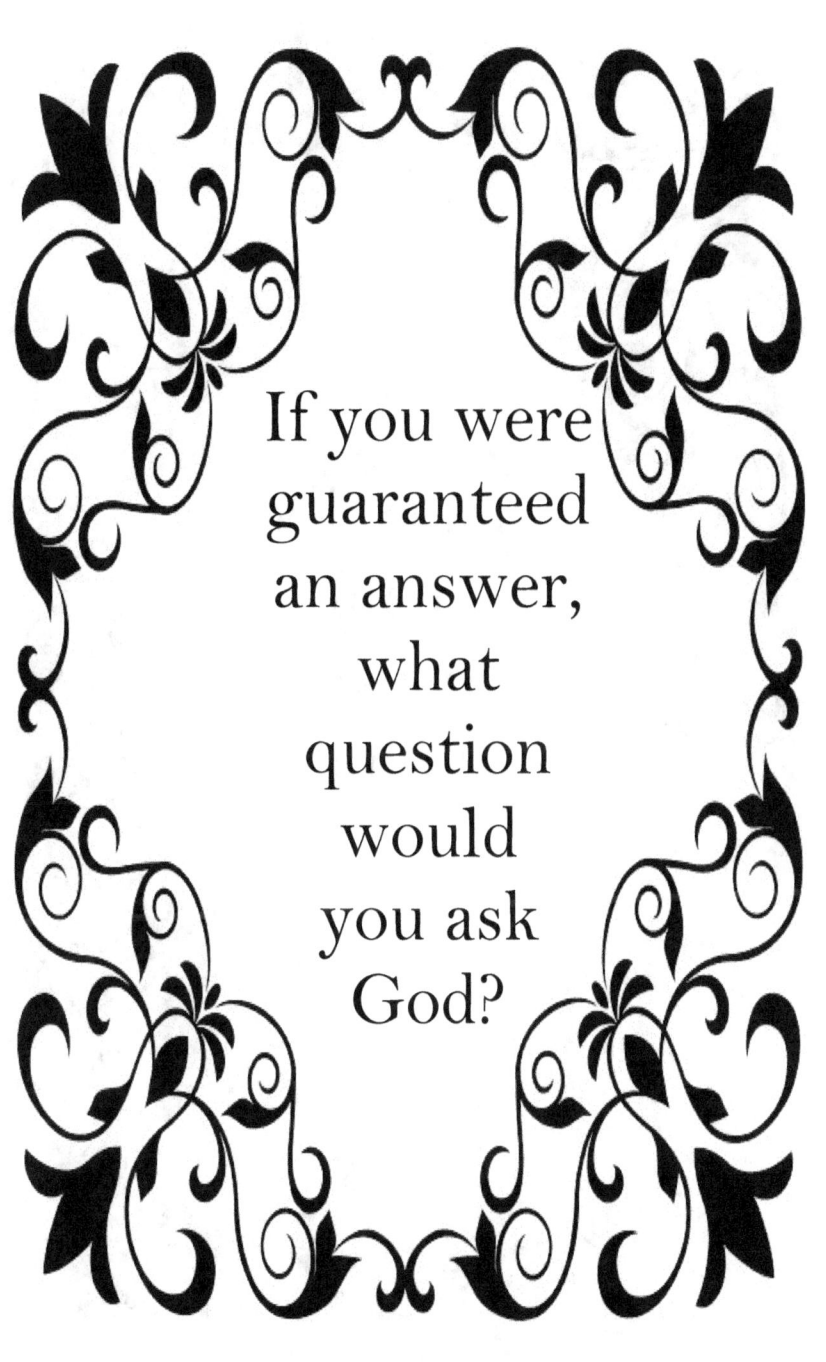

Describe your dream home.

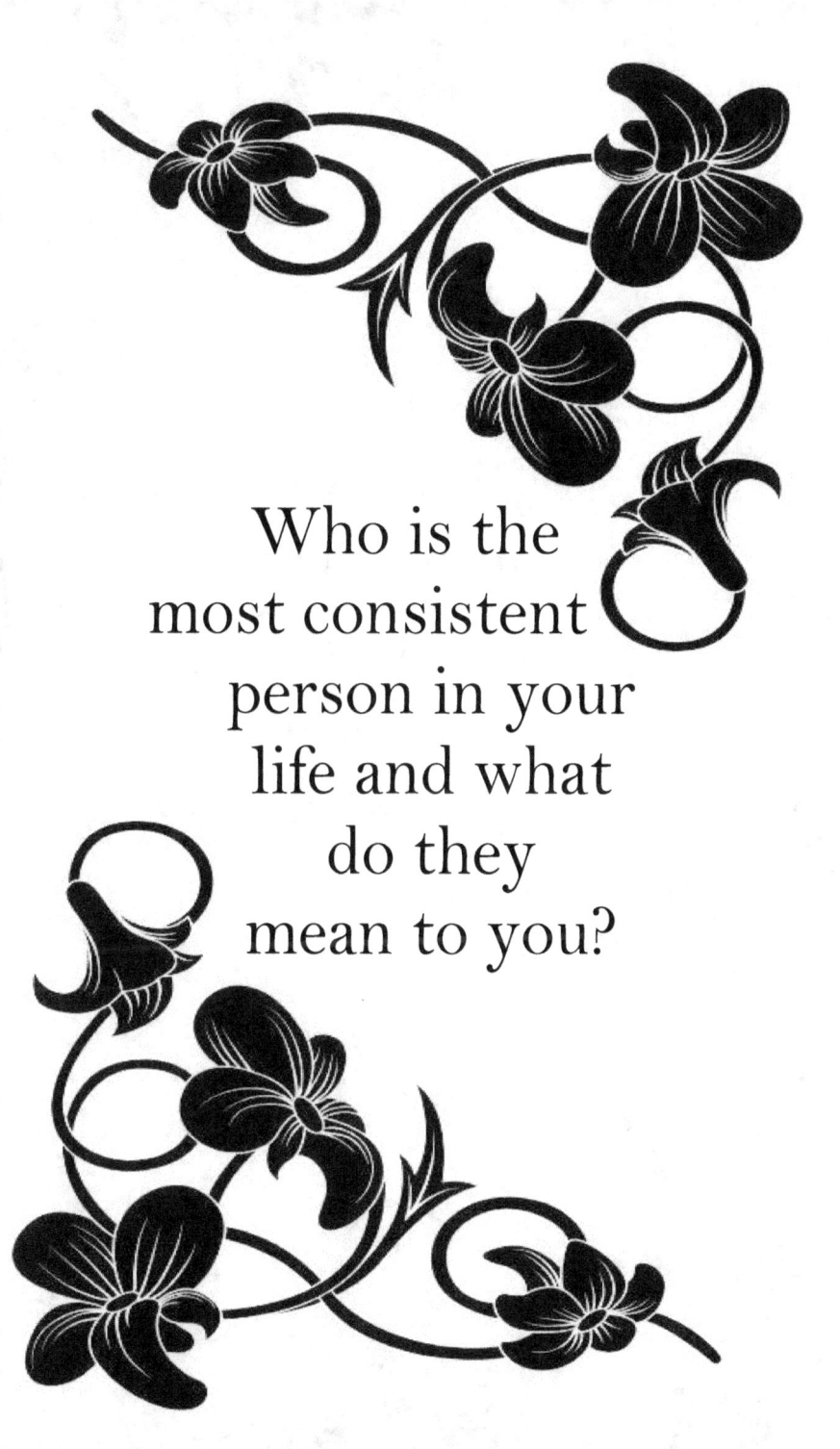

Who is the most consistent person in your life and what do they mean to you?

Describe your level of confidence in your ability to achieve your goals.

What will be the mark you leave on the world?

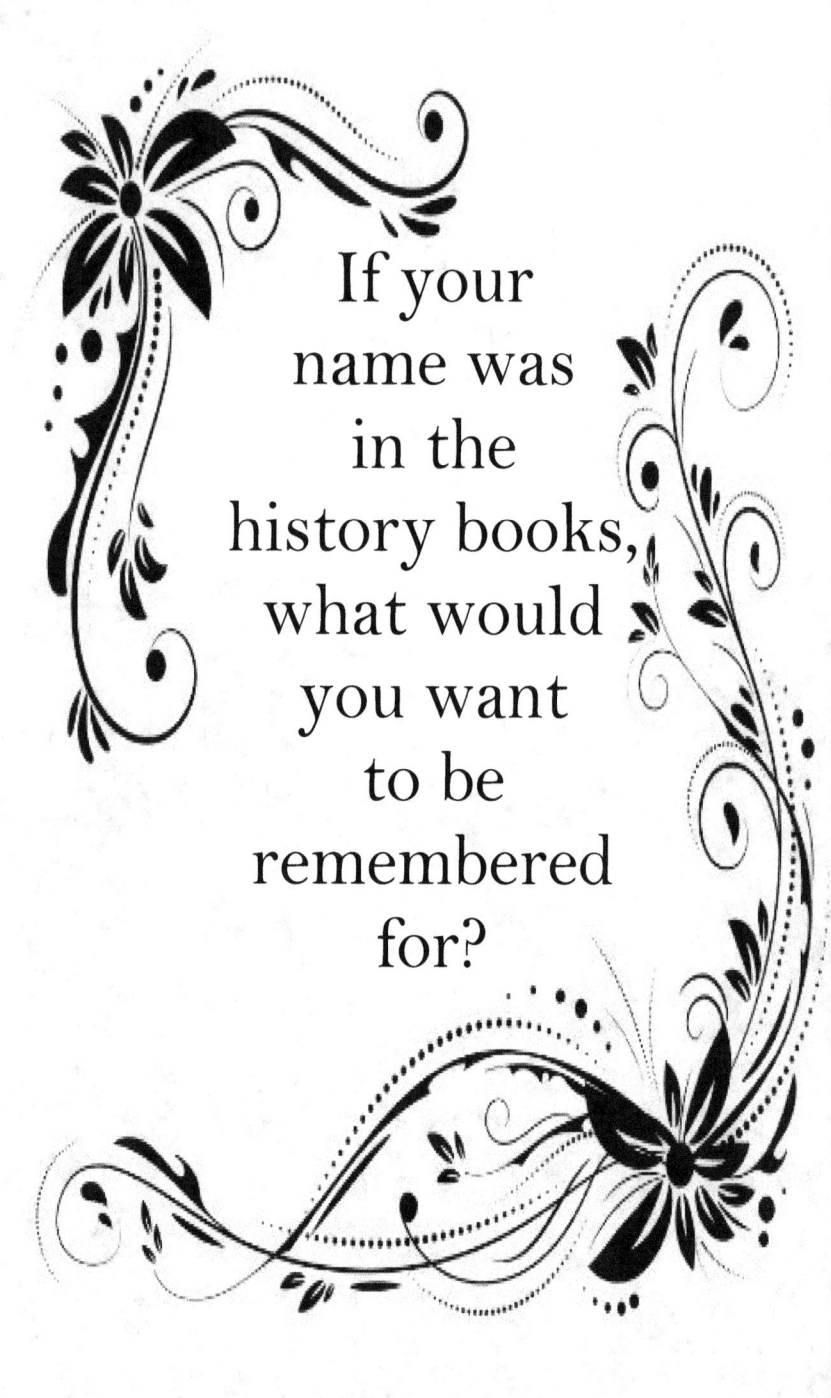

If your name was in the history books, what would you want to be remembered for?

What characteristics do you want in a friend?

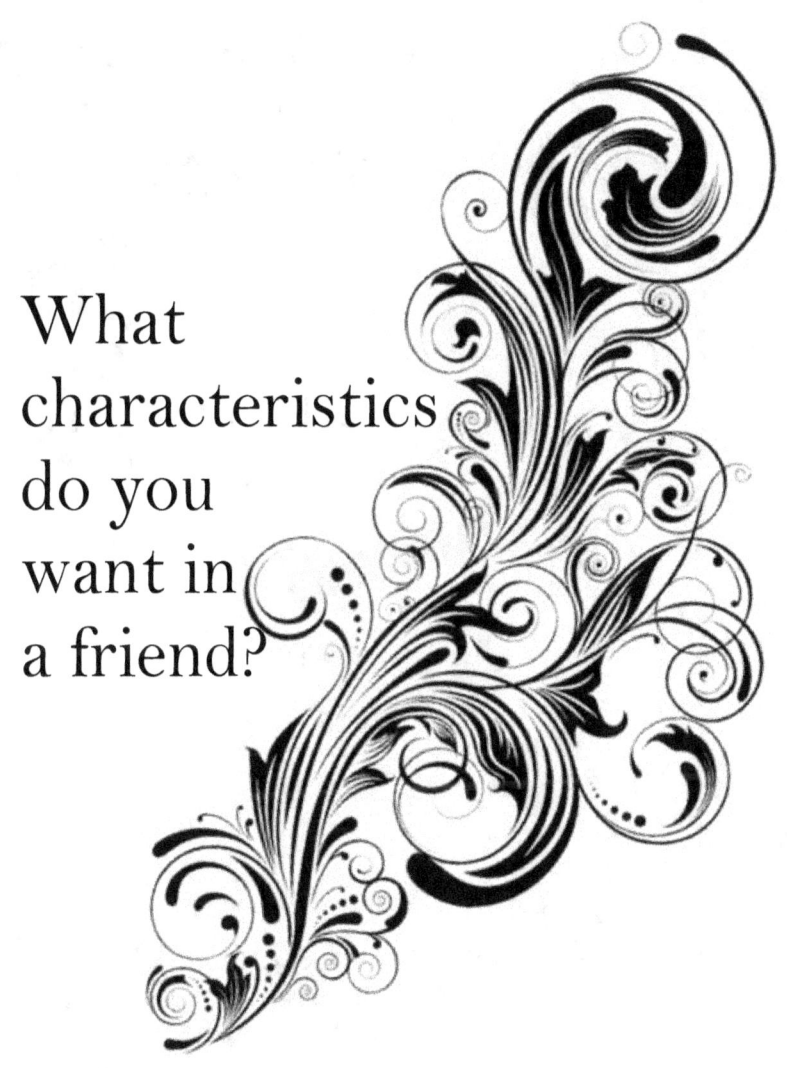

Tell me what worries you.

How do you typically respond to criticism? Explain.

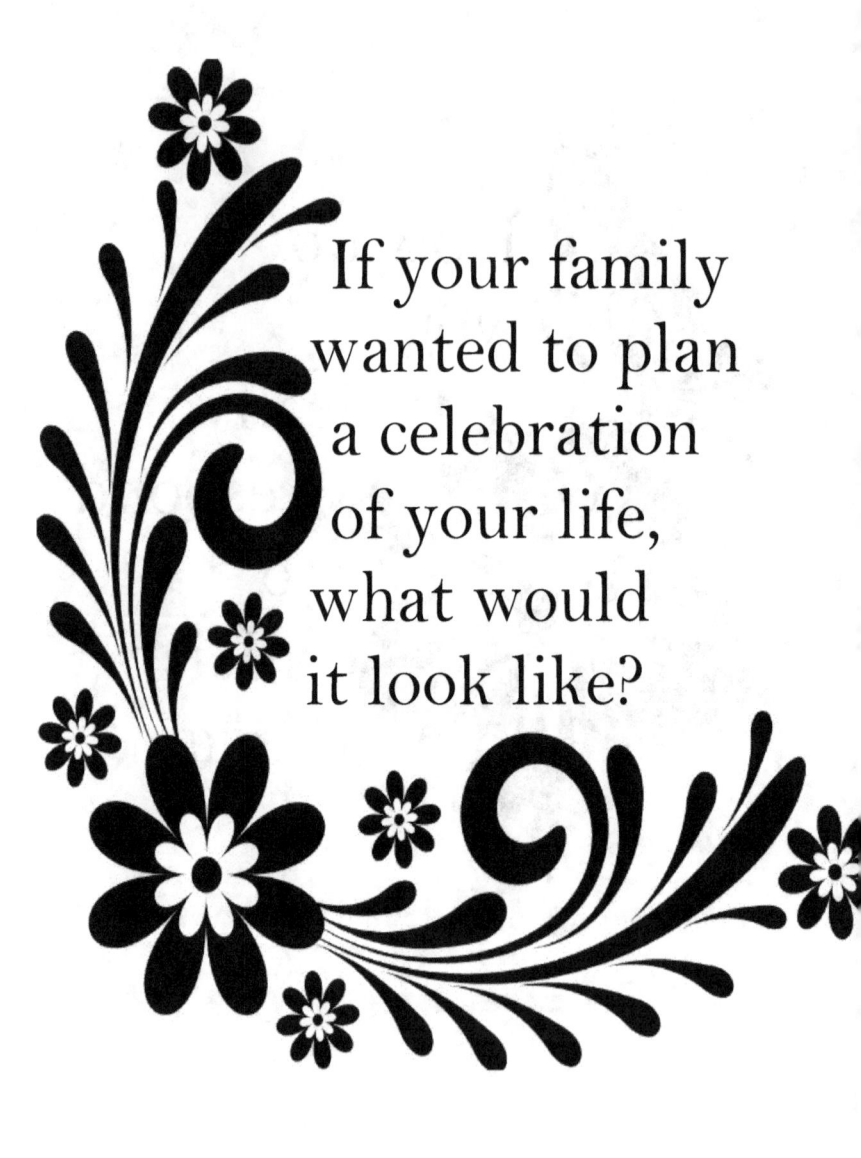

If your family wanted to plan a celebration of your life, what would it look like?

What advice would you give a college student who is considering dropping out?

Describe how you respond to changes in your life.

Tell me about a time where you felt appreciated.

What do you hope to leave as your legacy?

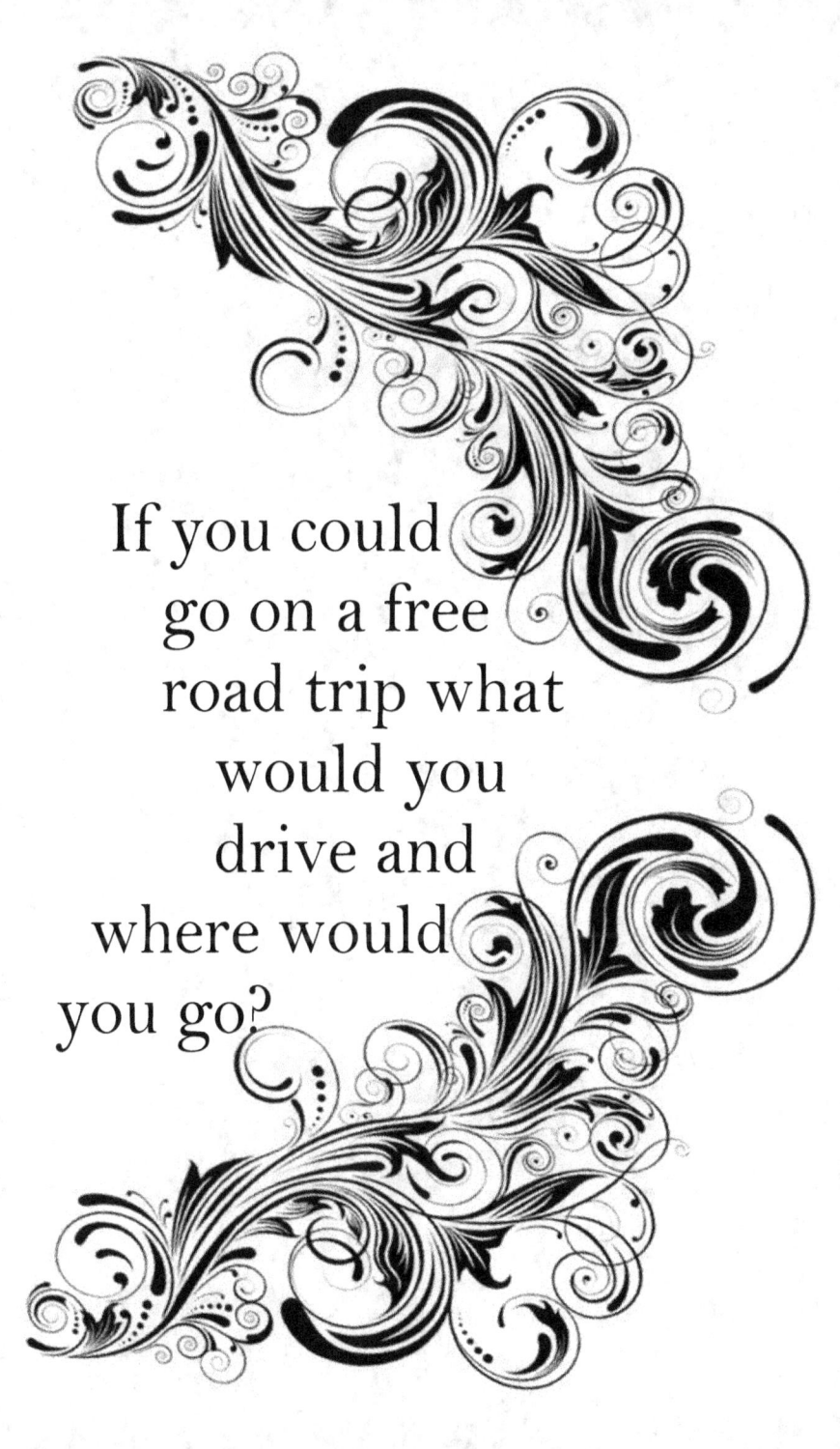

If you could go on a free road trip what would you drive and where would you go?

Write a letter to your childhood self.

Would you say you're a proactive or reactive person? Why?

What annoys you most about others?

How comfortable are you with expressing your emotions? Why?

What is keeping you from accomplishing all your dreams?

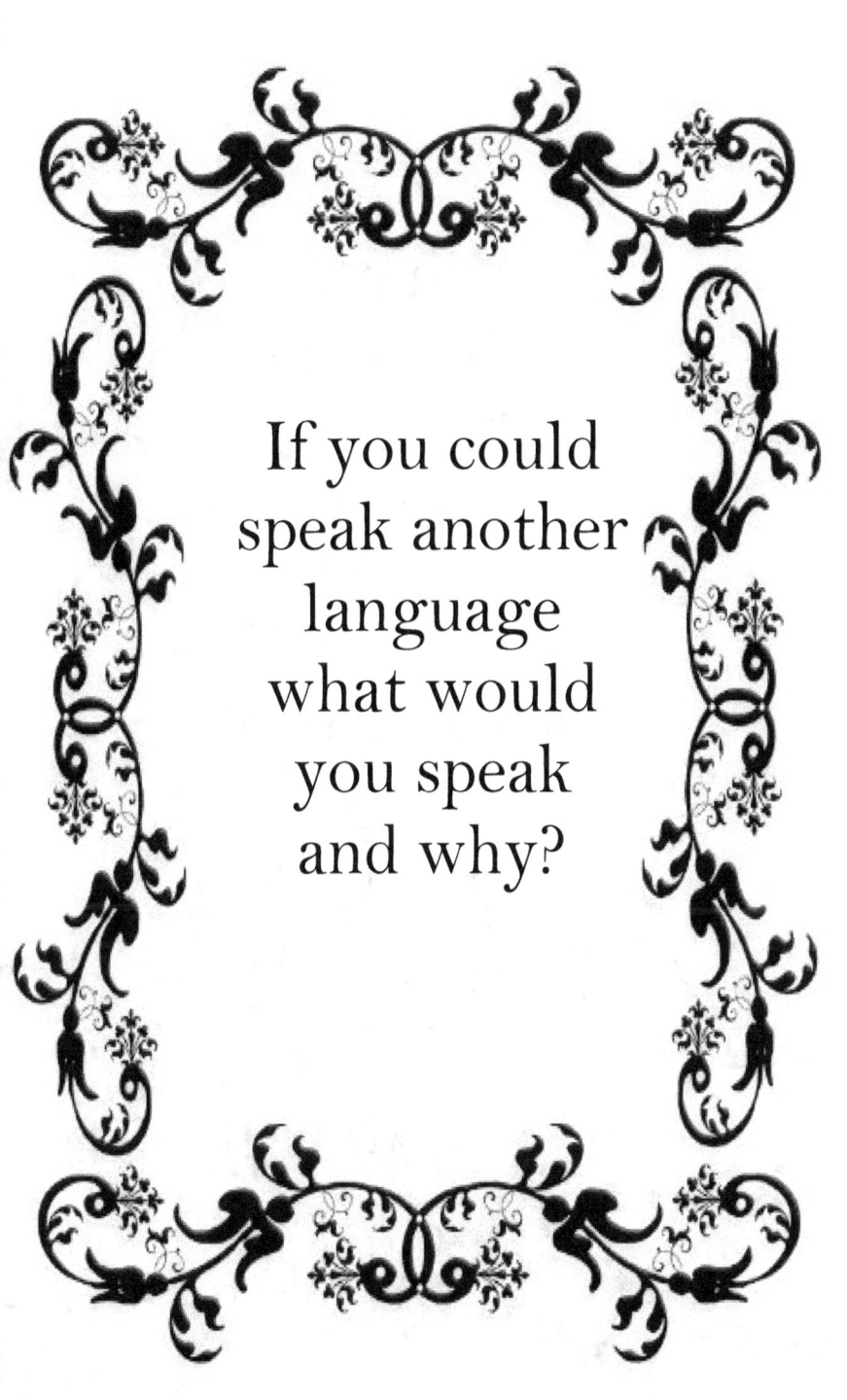

What do you love about your life?

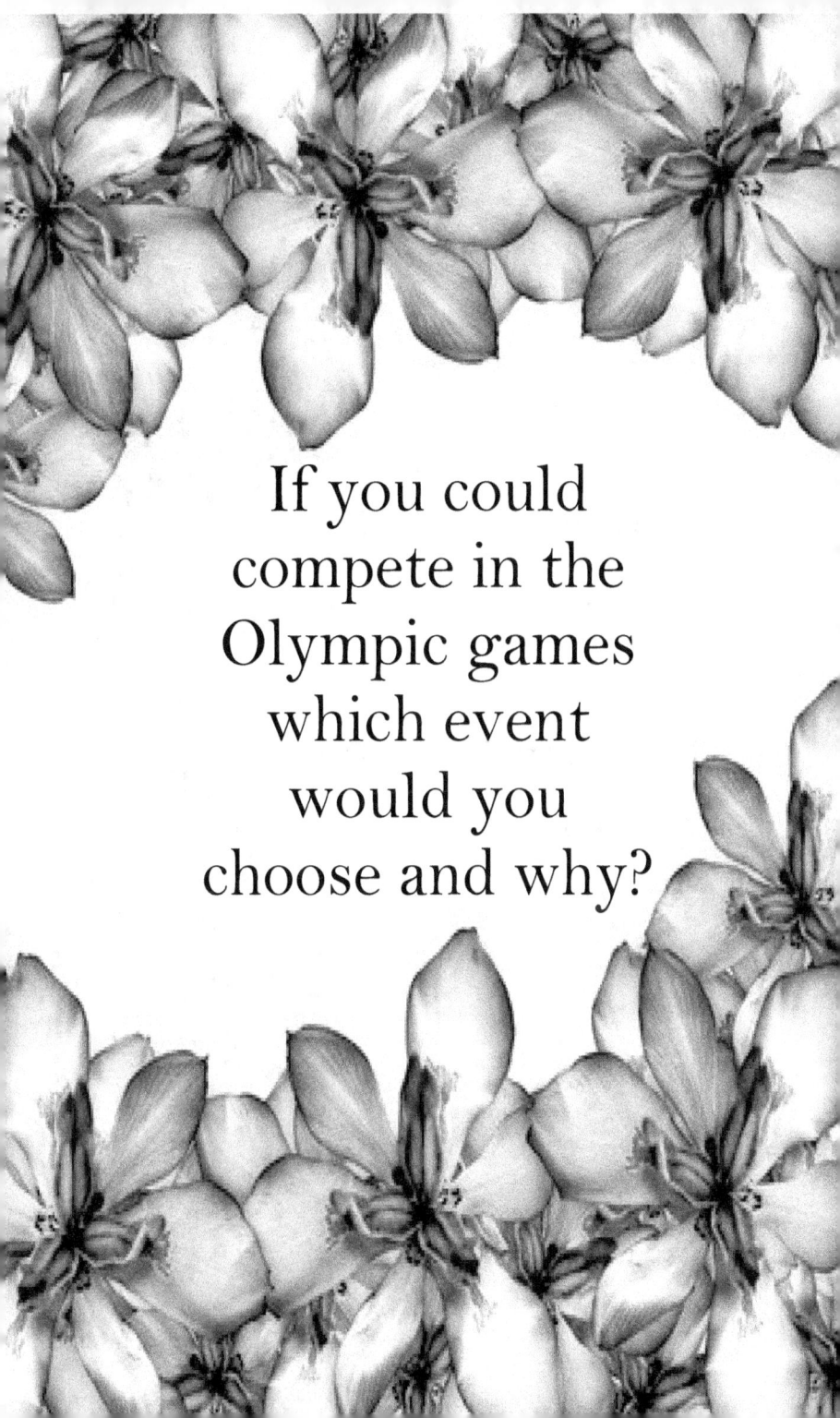

Would you consider yourself a perfectionist? Why or why not?

What was one of the hardest topics to talk to your parents about? Why?

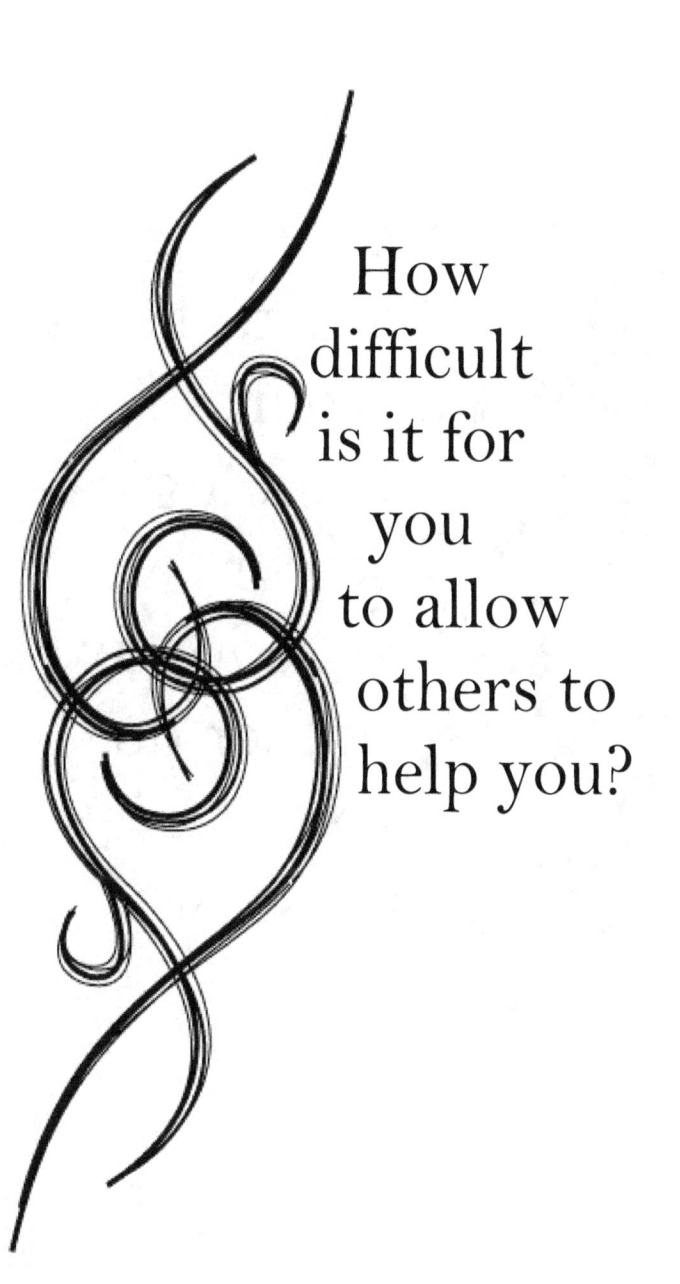

How difficult is it for you to allow others to help you?

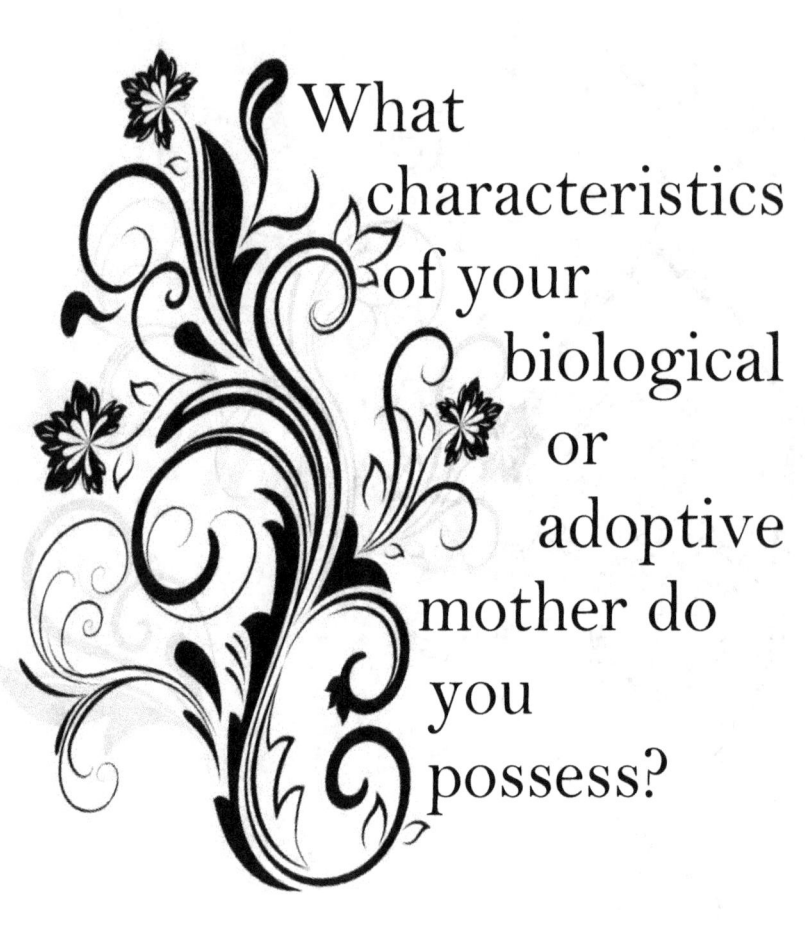

What characteristics of your biological or adoptive mother do you possess?

What advice would you give a child who is now experiencing life as you did?

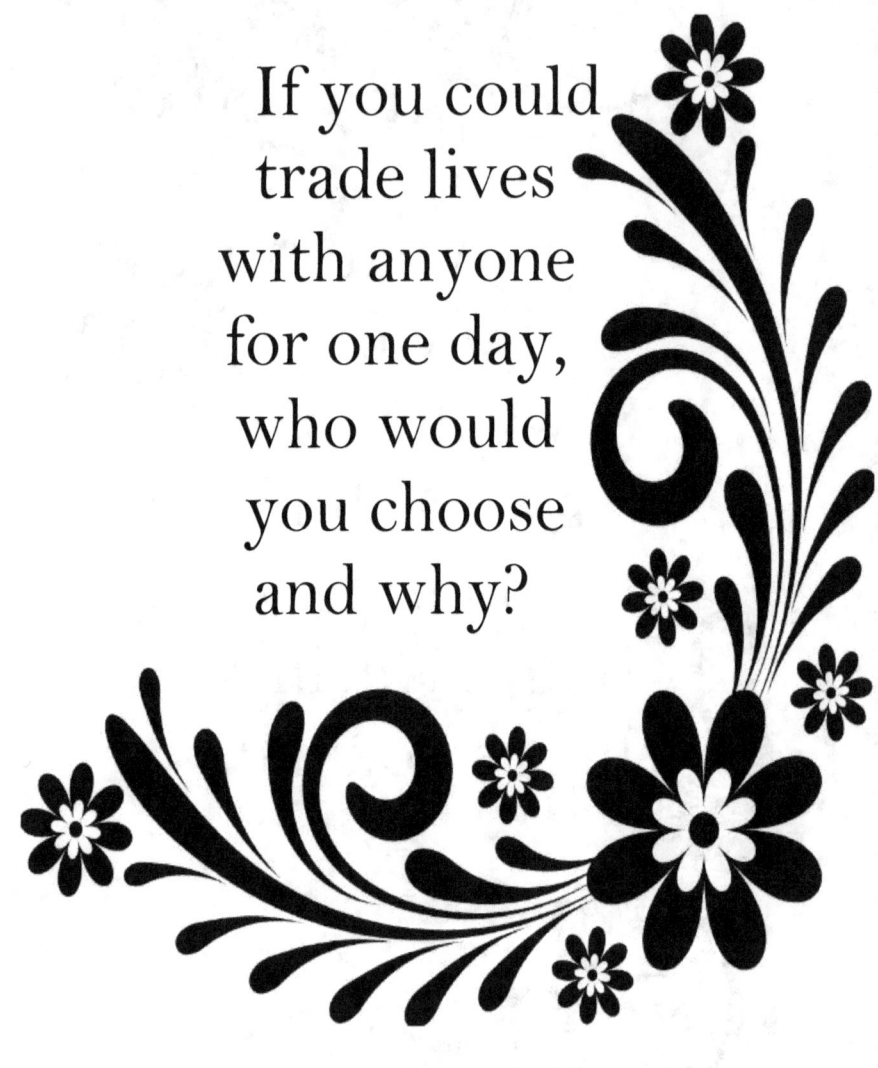

If you could trade lives with anyone for one day, who would you choose and why?

What's your favorite movie and why?

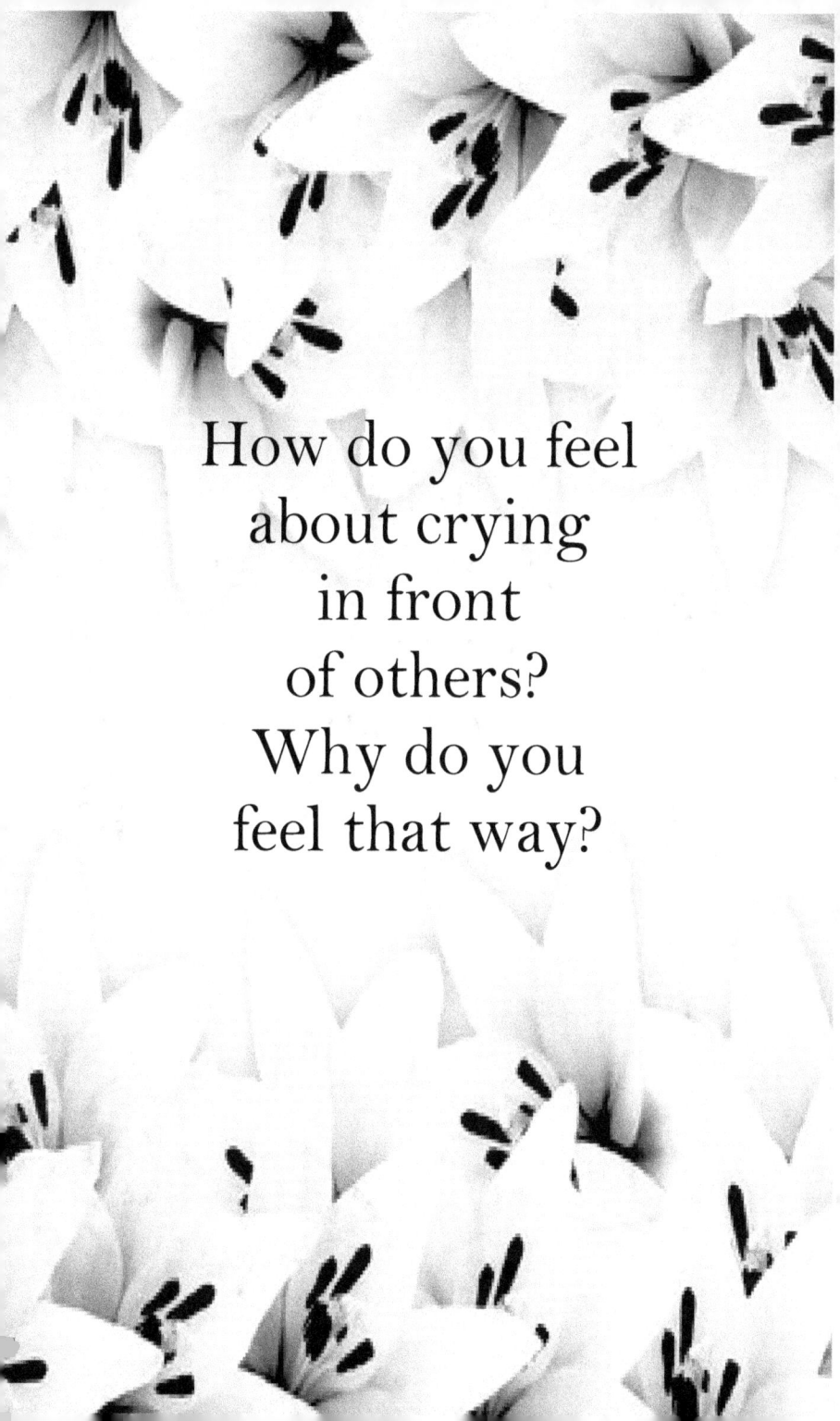

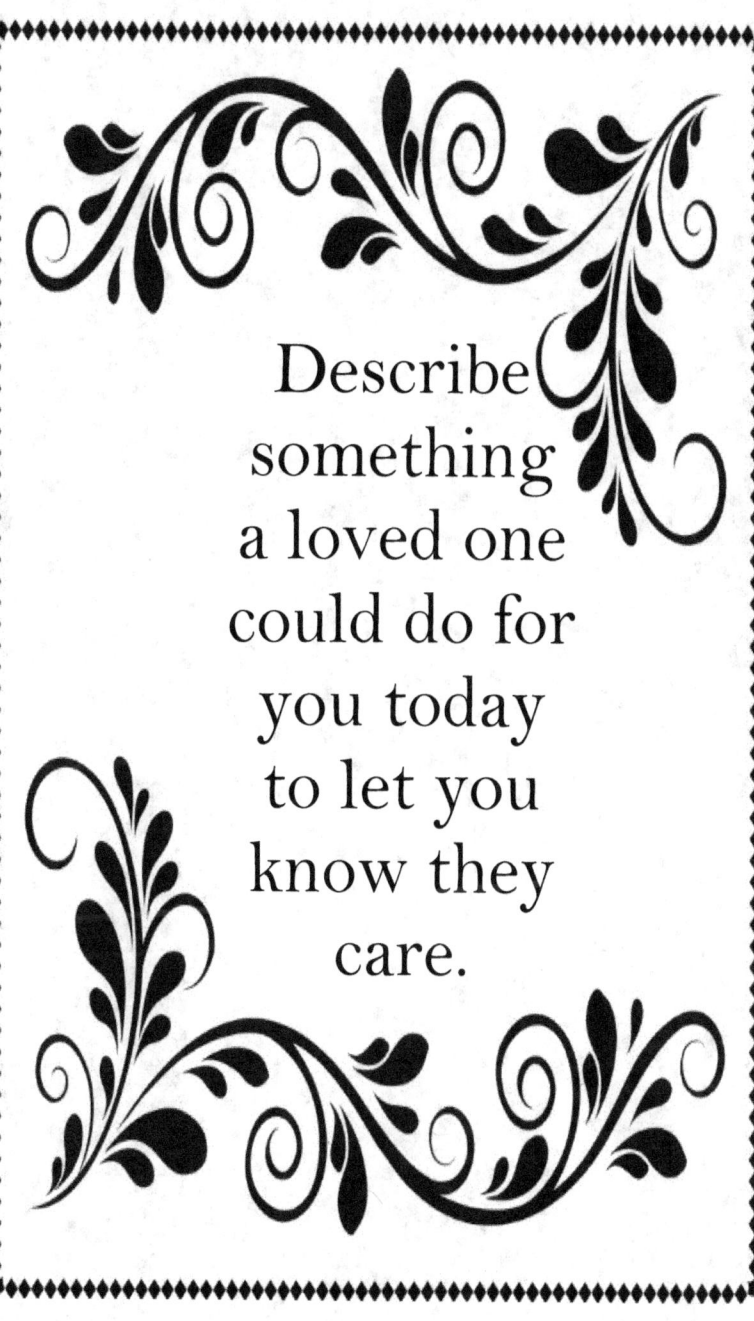

Describe something a loved one could do for you today to let you know they care.

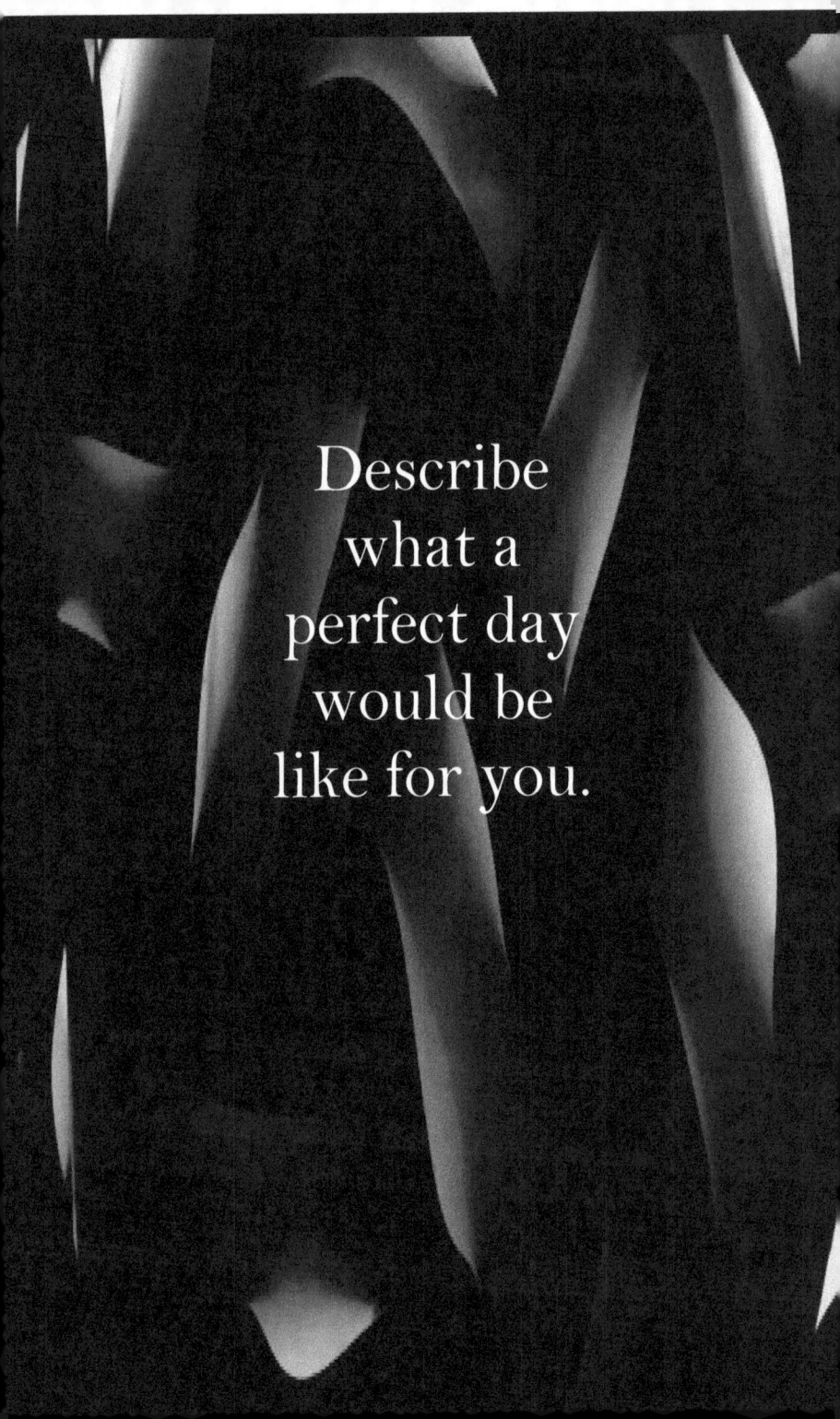

What mode of transportation (flying, driving, train, etc.) do you prefer and why?

Tell me one thing you find difficult to talk about or admit to yourself.

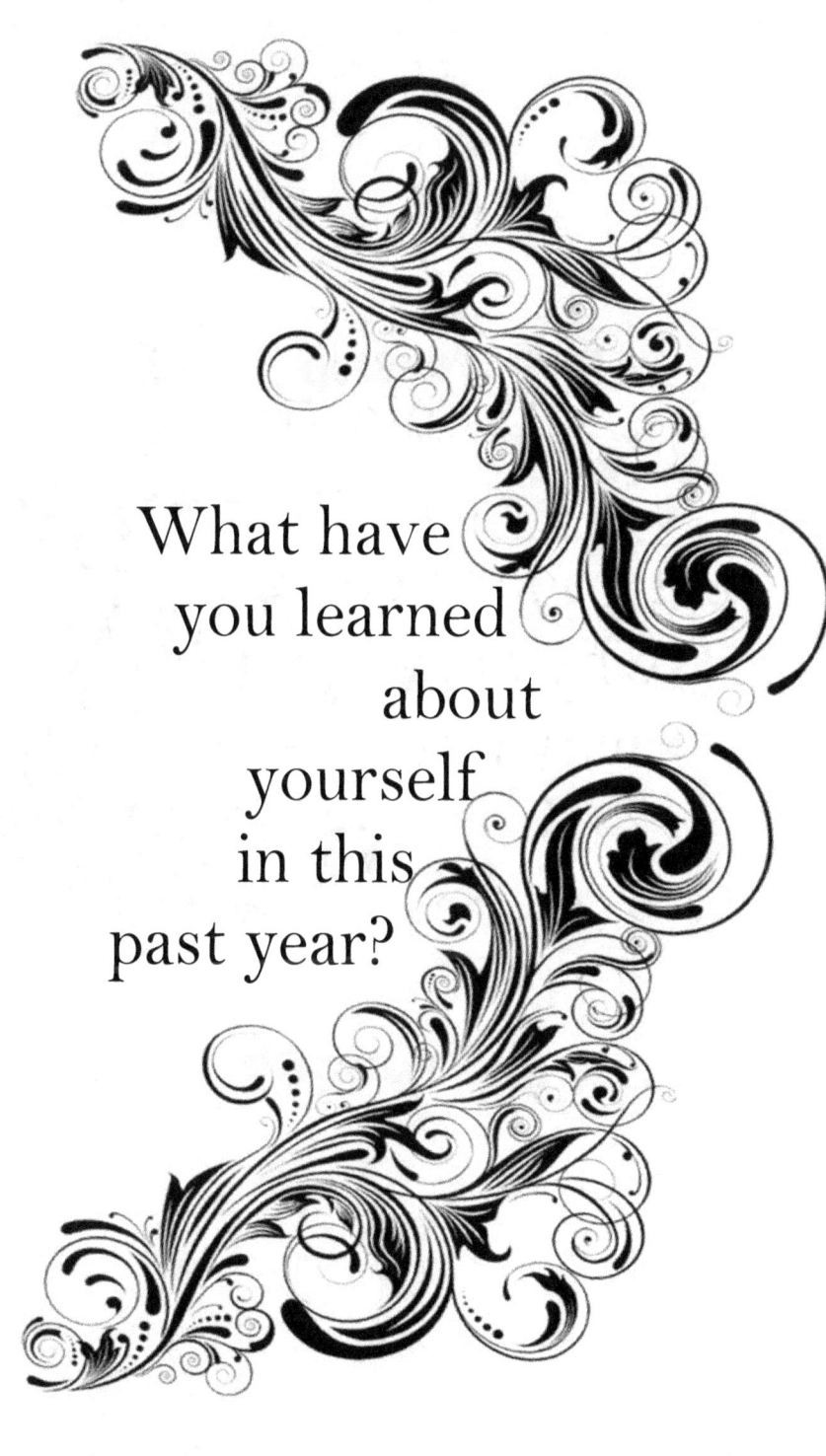

What have you learned about yourself in this past year?

Would you say you're a good friend? why or why not?

What are
your plans
for this
evening?

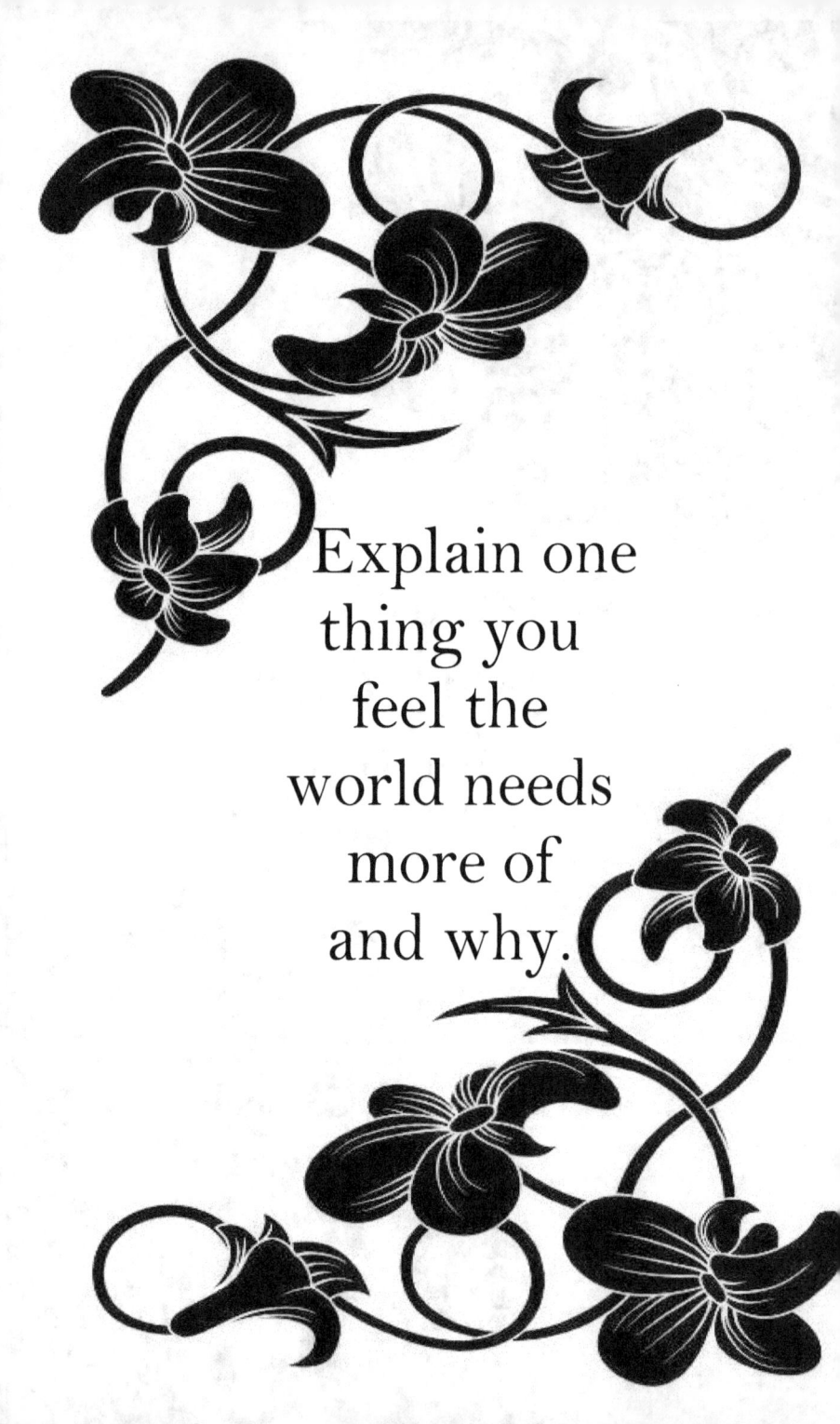

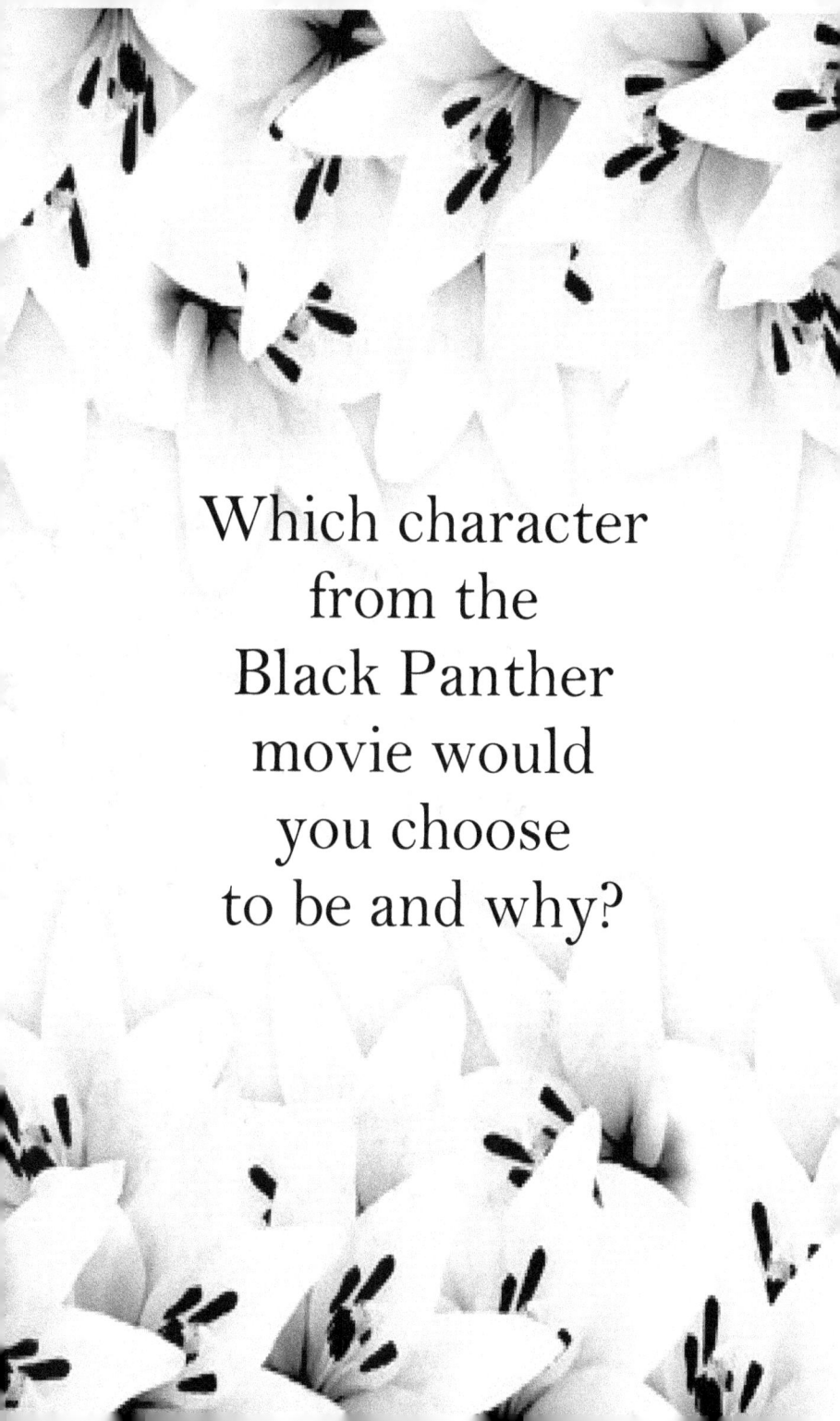

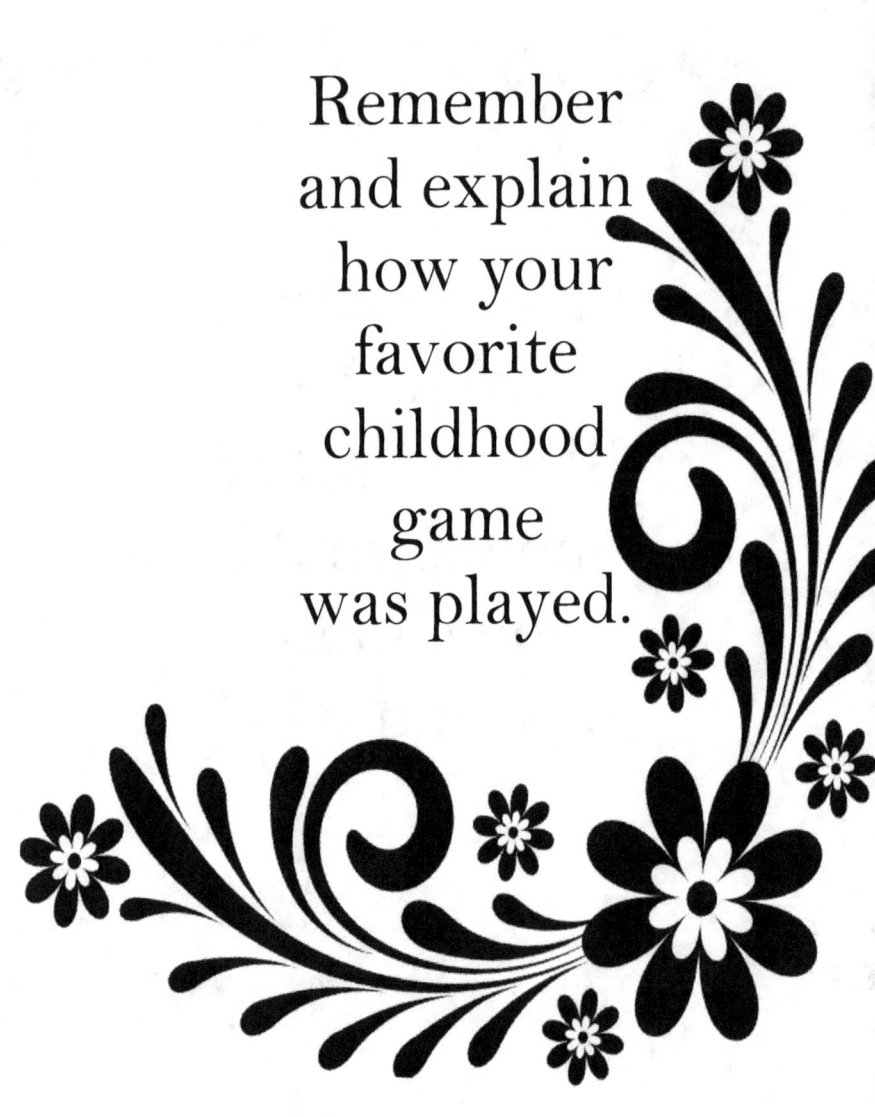

Remember and explain how your favorite childhood game was played.

Describe your gifts and talents.

Replay the best compliment you ever received.

What do you feel like you still need to learn about yourself?

What time of day are you most at peace and why?

What is one thing you would change about the way you were raised? Elaborate.

What's your favorite sport to watch or play? Why?

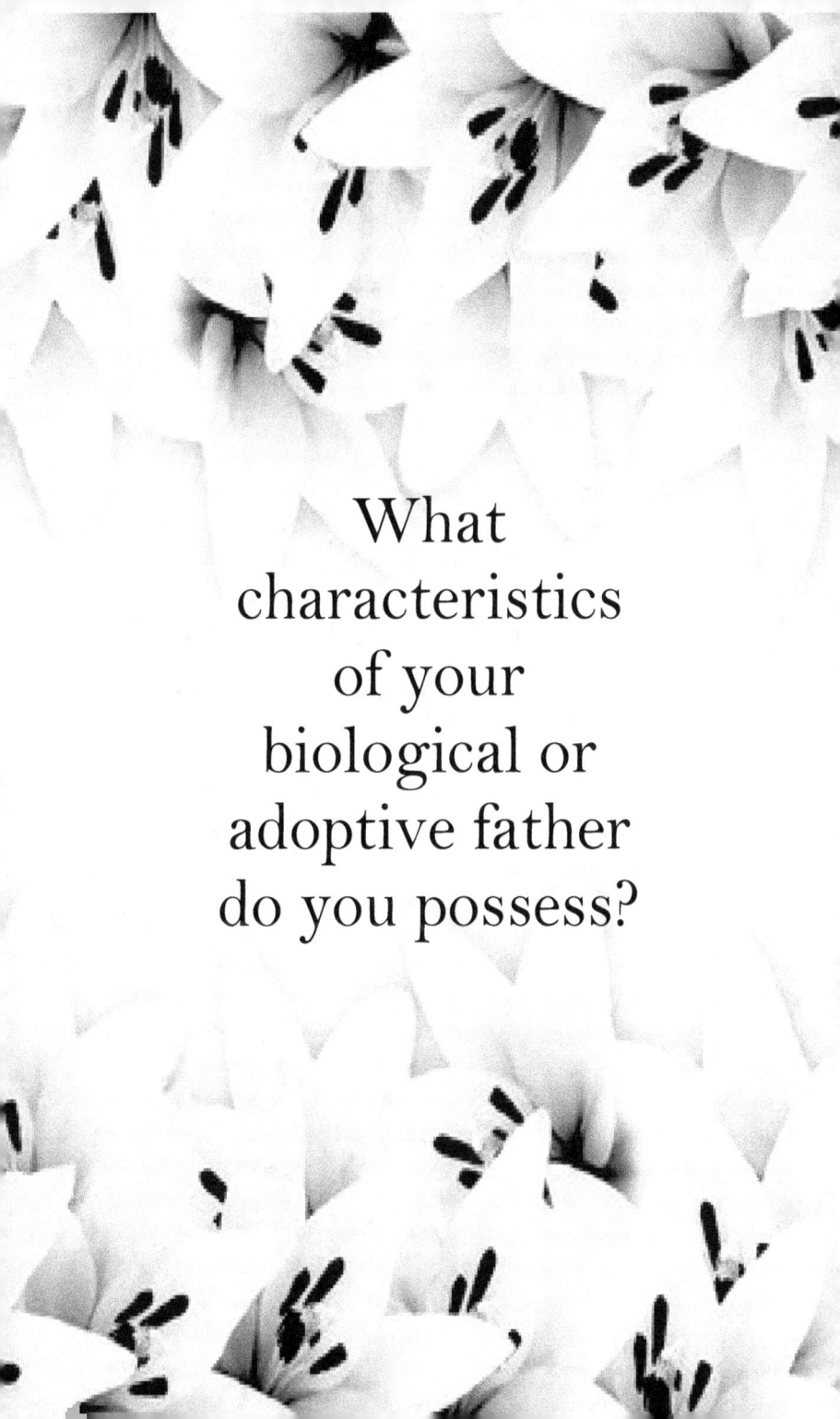

What characteristics of your biological or adoptive father do you possess?

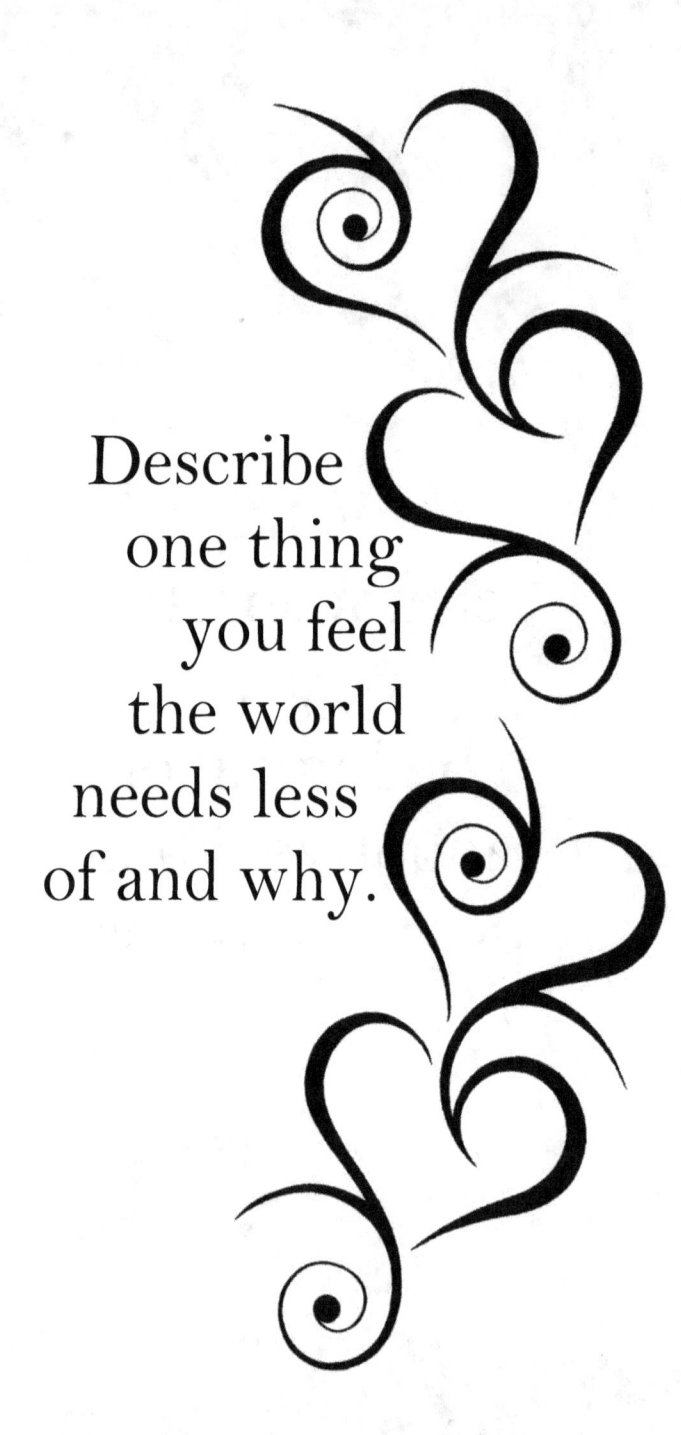

Describe one thing you feel the world needs less of and why.

What makes you feel at peace?

What season of the year do you enjoy most and why?

If you could star in a movie, what would be the movie title and why?

Describe your strengths.

Other Books By Soneakqua J. White

A Time to Heal

Red Flag!

Get Connected

Facebook.com/atthetablecounseling

Instagram.com/atthetablecounseling

YouTube.com/Author Soneakqua J. White

Visit her at www.soneakquajwhite.com

www.ingramcontent.com/pod-product-compliance
Lightning Source LLC
Chambersburg PA
CBHW052026070526
44584CB00016B/1922